The Story

of an

Intern

Ratnesh Dwivedi

ISBN: On the Back of Book

Front cover image by Ratnesh Dwivedi.

Book design by Ratnesh Dwivedi.

Printed by Create Space Inc.-An Amazon Company in the United States of America.

First printing edition 2012 by Zorba Publishers,Gurgaon,India.

 Publisher

Create Space Inc

USA

www.works.bepress.com/ratnesh_dwivedi

The greatest temptation journalists face is to regard the stories they write as their own. They are not, they are the stories of those who are involved in the events reported. It's not the journalist who is the hero, it is those who suffer famine or floods, those who fight cruelty or oppression, those who govern and those who oppose them. Never do I feel this more strongly than when I walk away from natural disasters with the material recorded for what I know will be 'a good story', leaving the victims to their sufferings.

Sir Mark Tully – Former Chief of Bureau, BBC in "No Full Stops in India"

Content

Foreword

."Each individual's life is a story, if penned beautifully then could be an inspiration for many" is the line which made me write my own story. Believe me, I avoided writing my story, starting from my birthplace, a rather spiritual but disputed place, Ayodhya, to the capital of India, but at last I found that there are some elements which must be heard by a section of society, hence I decided to write.

There have been many ups and downs in my life, many potholes and then some achievements which can be a story of any individual in your neighborhood. I was born in an aristocratic Brahmin family where education was given primary importance, but what it took for me to finally reach to my goal, was an unending story, a story that could have been a very personal experience in the big bad world of the media.

Many of us aspire to be an achiever but few make it their destiny. I do not know whether or not I have achieved something of value if we take into account an upbringing of a kid in the surroundings and atmosphere of a backward but rather religious town, which has seen the bloody battles over a temple cum mosque, later on changing the political destiny of the our country, but I must admit that in this journey I learnt something which is rare and remarkable.

It was all due to the support of my family, friends, people from all walks of life who I came across in this journey. They left an imprint on my life and helped me to finally gain shape from where I train and polish the new younger and bright generation.

The journey was tough and so was the traveler, as I often say, but experiences gained were exceptional.

From the tiny religious town of Ayodhya to my dream city Delhi where you often get lost on the way to achieving something and are are wrongly perceived by people of the big bad media world, I kept my head high through the a series of rejections, despair and disappointment, all thanks to a few people around me. In my way I saw stories of hope, courage, mysticism and misery in the wonderland that is India.

The instalments of this story may be great in number, but are kept short and precise and well connected with the next and will keep the travelers in this journey hooked and will enjoy their travels through all the potholes along with me.

People with whom I have met and who are the part of this journey are remarkable. They are unique in many a sense. **Ramchandra Paramhans** was one such individual who challenged the rigidity of the entire belief system on his rigidness for the glorious Ram temple to be built in

Ayodhya. His uniqueness in fighting and travelling together with Muslim counterparts is a lesson for many hardliners today. **Ami Vitale** is a remarkable photojournalist with lots of courage and hope. She has many times penetrated the remotest parts of the world alone in search of stories untold upto now. **Anita Pratap** was the first female head of CNN and the first to interview Velupillai Prabhakaran at his peak; she has been my inspiration. **Rajdeep Sardesai** has shaped today's TV journalism and I am thankful that we met at on a few occasions. Organizations like the BBC which supported me for two months and inspired me (not helped) to listen to the people who are part of the story. NASA also helped by providing some opportunities to attend its prestigious conferences. Places like Ayodhya, Delhi, Noida, Dehradun and Bangalore have been my home in this long battle and I will never forget to mention the stories of these places.

Then there are the people whose stories I have told in this journey. Myself as protagonist and all those who I came across along the way are themselves extremely readable material. I have tried to listen and tell the stories of all those who left an imprint in my life.

I must admit also that in the various instalments that will be published, you will find the stories of all shades of life. My elder brother has been my sole source of support through the dark days and long battles with joblessness. My parents who gave me birth and helped me fight this battle are also my mentors. My wife has given me a lot of time and patience to share my difficulties as has my infant son.

I am thankful to all who inspired me to write this wonderful *Story of an Intern.*

Wishing you the very best on this journey.

Ratnesh Dwivedi

March 2012,Noida

Beginning of the Journey

This is the story of deep pain and shallow gains. This is the story of an unending journey which has shown me all the ups and downs, suffering and pleasure, sorrow and happiness in media and has made me emerge from the darkness into an enlightened world, one that has transformed me from an infant to a fully grown man in the media.

I recall my meeting with a rather low profile, but remarkable achiever in media, Madhukar Upadhyaya, when I had just passed my 10th board exam in 1990. He was in Ayodhya to cover the bloody shoot out on the streets and I, by that time, had decided to make my way in journalism. That was a very cool meeting at his native house amidst long tall trees, a holy temple and an old but in all directions building. As I entered his house through an old creaking and trembling stairway he came out in a 'lungi' with a 'Janeu' on his bare upper abdomen. Very politely he said, *"Thakur pandit ji ke bete ho."* I gave a positive nod and then discussed my dream to be like him and serve in the three letter charisma of media, the BBC. He wrote down his Delhi home address and promised to meet me there after my graduation.

Exactly five years later, when I passed the entrance test for a Mass Communication course at University of Lucknow University I again rang him to ask whether or not to submit the fee for said course, at which point he advised me to stick with it, which then decided my fate to pack up my bags for a rather longer journey in the media. The year was 1997 and the month was March.

Lucknow University, as I had presumed, had nothing much to offer in terms of classroom studies, but as a city Lucknow at that time was the 'Mecca of the Media,' for it was a center for all kind of politics that we were studying. So, soon after taking admission in the Masters program, and to live up to my father's dream, I started roaming around and knocking on the doors of each newspaper and media house. Luckily, I was noticed by one of my teachers and a veteran in the media, Karuna Shanker Saxena, who offered me the opportunity to write on a regular basis for a feature agency, where he was serving as editor.

It was a kick start to my career in the media alongside my studies and I truly enjoyed my job which lasted for six months, up to my departure from Lucknow to Delhi. The first article I wrote was on Chinese leader Deng-Xiaoping's death and was published, not rejected. I developed relationships in the *Hindustan Times* and visited its Lucknow office several times. I recall that we had plenty of students crazy about journalism and some of them have come a long way. Indeed beginning in journalism was as I had predicted. People with long beards and empty bellies walking into a newspaper office to get their sarticles published and editors always trying to find out how to reject them!

Through these unforgettable experiences, and as time rolled on, a year had passed, but somewhere deep in my conscience was the picture of Delhi, where the real media war was being fought. This was the war between fresher and experienced media people, the war between print and electronic journalism, the war between vernacular language and English journalism and a war which has really given the shape to today's media industry through the efforts of the real heroes who are no longer with us...

And I got my way, I got the opportunity to knock on Delhi's doors, as I always say *'where there is a will there is a way.'*

Igor Ovsyannykov photo

Lucknow and Journalism

My story is still focused in Lucknow. As I said, the Department of Mass Communication and Journalism at Lucknow University had nothing much to offer but the people in and around were interesting in many ways and must get a place in this story....

Dr R C Tripathi, HOD as he likes to be refered to, is a man who cultivated his father's legacy, to hold the flagship post. He was a typical Hindi man surrounded with only 'likeminded people'. He was the sole man to run the department and his strength was the veteran man who nourished all of us. We all were dependent on our guest faculties who trained and polished us.

Girish Mishra, a journalist with the number one Hindi daily, and who perhaps has never compromised his principles, put forward an insightful view of reporting. Then there was Akhilesh Mishra, another veteran in 'Gerua Kurta-Dhoti' who taught us 'Press Law'. Most of the laws, of press, supreme court rulings, the Constitution of India and political systemwere at his fingertips.

But as I said, I rather used my time after the classes to search for a freelance job, which I got in due course. The department had some amazing students, one an aged Muslim friend, Hassan Ejaz from Aligarh. I have never seen such an enthusiastic and eager to learn fellow with a mastery over the Islam religion.

Pradeep Nair, who later stuck around the department, was another bookworm, who was seldom humiliated by another friend of mine, Ashvini Bishnoi. Ashivini to whom I referred as 'Ashvini Albela, Lakhon Mein Akela' was a staunch Hindi supporter who possessed a dominating attitude. He was smart and popular and had a keen interest in girls,he had a cutting edge with his presence of mind.

Mukul Srivastava, who later became a Ph.D holder under Dr Tripathi and is now the only permanent faculty in the department, had a witty and sharp tongue, always pinning me down with his jokes that were crafted only for me.

Bhavna and Sarika were lady attractions in our batch. Bhavna was pretty good in communicating and we talked at few occasions.Sarika later shifted her base to Mumbai.Yogesh Dixit was our senior, and is now serving with the *Hindustan Times* group at a senior level. Anwar was the only office assistant-cum-photographer in the department.

And with this powerful team the department was running with all its might. And amidst all this, there was me who was desperately looking to make it in the media, in the politically warm city of Delhi, my efforts resulting in getting published in several newspaper's feature pages and a couple of jobs offered on a part-time basis.

In addition there were also our late sittings in Lekhraj Towers to have 'parathas' and our point of focus on girls at Ashvini's house, our search for news and current affairs magazines, Manorma year book and literature books. Ashvini's preference was the Civil Service and now I hope he has made it.

'Ganzing' (roaming in Hazrat Ganj–Lucknow's Heart) was also a daily routine. And there was my attempt to overshadow all of it, for which I seemed to have had 'Obsessive-Neurosis-Disorder'.

But I was hungrier and was often dreaming of Delhi.

So, I got my way by securing a place in the Post Graduate Diploma in Journalism Program of Delhi University, though I never finished it and returned to the University of Lucknow program.

I remeber when Ashvini came to my rented room three hours in advance and even came to Charbagh Railway Station to help me board the Lucknow mail. And as the train caught speed and made me move faster towards the Media City, Delhi, Lucknow, the city by that time, had left a lifetime imprint, never to be forgotten on me. The year was 1997, the month September.

Into the Jat Land and South Campus

My first impression I had of Delhi was of a city of 'Jats' with a tough tounge in their mouth and a lathi in their hand. But it was also an impression of a city which is the best at imparting education. The first impression though was overshadowing the last. Hence I decided to break my journey in Ghaziabad and landed in a small apartment of my relatives.

The very next day I had to submit my fees to the South Campus of Delhi University and took a DTC bus from ALT to Shiva Ji Stadium, Cannaught Place. I thought that after one hour long journey I would have reached DU, but I was still only in the middle of my journey as confirmed by a DU girl sitting on the adjacent seat. I was in the heart of the capital of India and was required to change the bus, so again took bus no. 620 which penetrated the Ring Road at Moti Bagh passing through India Gate, Chankya Puri and Shanti Path. Here I was able to visit some pictursque monuments and places of Delhi.

Anyhow I changed the bus again and took a Mudrika Ring Road sewa to Dhaula Kuan and entered the South Campus of Delhi University.

The department was and still is in bad shape. Much to my shock it was the poorest department in all the universities running Mass Communication courses and since it was attached to the Hindi Department, the administration hardly cared about it. There was no permanent faculty and with just an office assistant, Pradeep Budhiraja, and a vetearn academician and HOD of DU's Hindi Department ,Prof Nityanad Tiwari, was administered.

The very same moment I introduced myself to Mr Budhiraja, I decided that I was not going to finish the course and would certainly go back to Lucknow University. But I had to save my back. I found myself unable to tell my father, where I was actually stuck, so I decided to face the challenge.

Also there was a charm to being in Delhi and its powerful media circle, which was my priority. So to get an excuse to remain in Delhi and meet its media people, I joined the course.

The second big challenge was to find a cheap and good room in a nearby location. Hence I started weighing my options and running around to find the right accommodation...

I spent the initial two months with a military family in Delhi Cantt. It was nice seeing India's defense forces and its amazing people walking around. But my hunt for an independent shelter continued. While on the way to South Campus from Delhi Cantt one day, a person told me about localities in Palam Vihar and Mahipalpur. So after the classes I searched out this place near IGI airport on NH-8. The place, a 'Jat' village, metamorphoses into a rich village with a five star hotel Radison in its surroundings and the IGI airport two kms away; unique in many a sense.

I landed up in one house asking for a cheap room room at a cheaper rate. The fat lady asked for Rs.1000 Rs/month but I finally negotiated it for on Rs. 750 per month. The most attractive thing were the tiny dhabas just outside the village (let's not call it a village as it had the above features in its surroundings) and awesome people in it. The first time I saw the Jat culture I instantly liked it. I firmly believe that this community can never be changed whatsoever. They are born to dominate.

The room was shared by one of my fellow classmates who later left as he got another cheaper room.

This is the place which changed my perception towards life and really cultivated an attitude which was never liked by others. However I regained my 'sophisticated behavior', which is my weak defeating point to date.

I still miss Mahipalpur and its people, a lot.

Manoj Dubey was the man who phoned me first about my selection in the DU course and he was the first man to make me feel stuck about the student lobby in DU. A man in his early thirties and a civil services aspirant, he joined the course to leave an option in case he did not get selected in IAS. However he never succeeded in his goal and I do not know where he is and how far he has travelled in the media.

Brajesh Mishra, a young boy from Patna with a humorous personality and a relaxed approach towards the media, was the second person who caught my attention. He was my fellow traveller in the journey through the media and even interned with me in *ZEE news*. He is a tall man, always liked by the girls, and he made me laugh whenever I found it hard to make it in the media. I never saw such an energetic fellow who achieved success at an early stage. He is now working as Bureau Chief of Patna bureau of Zee News.

Next is the story of Manish Kumar Jha, a man who never gave up whatsoever no matter what kind of difficulties he faced. He was staying in Munirka village in a tiny room, almost half of which was occupied by tons of books, all paperbacks and published by Raj Kamal. Name a Hindi book and it was there in his room.

And then there was Vikram Sharma, a man who was from the lot of goalless creatures in south campus where he roamed around without even bothering to enrol in any course. A staunch RSS supporter, I saw him arguing within each and every corner of south campus on any issue which involved even a tiny mention of RSS. I admired his cynicism.

And then there was a lobby of civil service aspirants which was very regular to south campus just for the sake of the library. The head of this lobby was Suresh Vashistha, a bald man who always looked like he was in his late thirties and never like a civil service aspirant. He later made it to the top 20 list of IAS, who went the way of LBS in Mussoorie.

Sarvada Nand, how I can forget a man who was always trying to impress you without any reason, always intorducing himself with a soft voice; (however he never succeeded in it). Sarvada was in the Cold War era with Suresh Vashishtha but as I said, he never succeeded as Suresh had a long fan following in the South Campus.

Amidst all this, there was me, a rather young boy who, in whatever way was always busy making dozens of calls to media persons, editors and correspondents to meet him in order to get a foothold in the media.

The cynicism and persistence of making phone calls, sooner, was going to give him results...

Very soon, we all turned the South Campus into our second home. It became our shelter for the day and sometimes even for the night (an unofficial residence for some of us). It was only here we discovered what we had to choose to decide our destiny.

As for me, I converted it into a mini office for myself, especially the yellow phone booth inside the arts faculty building and the PCO just close to its gate.

The first phone call I made was to Madhukar Upadhyaya. As soon as I rang him on his BBC number, a soft voice transfered the call to him. Many of us across the listenership of the BBC Hindi Service might agree about the magical pitch, intensity and volume (we studied all the characters on voice modulation of his voice. "Hello" he uttered. I held my breath and asked him for his permission to give me an appointment to meet him in his office.

And as promised some eight odd years back, he agreed and called me at 3pm the very next day. This might turn into a decisive moment, I thought. I collected all my paper clipings which I had published in Lucknow, my certificates (this was a common practice for me whenever I got a chance to meet any significant person to show my 'might' through certificates – I don't know if I ever succeeded in my attempt) and reached at 3:15, late by a full fifteen minutes.

He was busy writing his script (news story) and with his magical smile, very politely reminded me that I was late. With all my courage and softness I asked him to give me a chance for an internship at the BBC. I am still not sure to this day what he had said, but when I came out of the office the beautifully crafted receptionist smiled at me. And it was then I realized I was going to spend a couple of months in the magical realm of the BBC and its marvelous people.

This was the beginning of my cynicism in making phone calls, collecting phone numbers and asking the media giants to give me an opportunity, which I now feel has developed into my weak point as I felt that I was begging for something. There is a saying 'beggars can't be choosers have no choice.'

I am sure that as far as people in the media are concerned there are only two male exceptions where this 'beggar' phenomenon did not appy, these being Madhukar Upadhyaya and Rajdeep Sardesai.

Yes, the ladies in the media were always my inspiration, whosoever came my way.

The next call I made was to Rahul Dev (a man with whom I opted to meet thirteen times, and at every time he agreed) and to Nalini Singh's office.

Not to say the South Indian man and his beautiful canteen inside the South Campus had been feeding me and even intentionally still asking me whether or not I had got my lunch. Murthy's canteen had been a place from where I bought my lunch everyday, and sometimes dinner too. I do not know the reason. Was it good food or Murthy's affection? I do not know if I still owe a debt of at least a thousand to him!...

Phone calls, Meetings with Biggies and Thunder Bolt

Rahul Dev, at that time, was heading a program which by then had created waves in Indian media circles, and every journalist was willing to take a chance during that half hour of charisma in the Indian Television News industry.

Aaj Tak, conceptualised and designed by the late Mr Surendra Pratap Singh, was a half an hour current affairs and news show on *DD Metro* that had become a destination point for many of today's achievers in the media. Surendra Pratap Singh was a man who had created history as the editor of the *Nav Bharat Times* and Anand Bazar Patrika Ravivar at a very early stage of his life as a journalist. A man without any bias, he was an articulate journalist, and moreover a good human being. He died of a brain heomopharage in 1997. I never got a chance to meet him sadly.

Rahul Dev was his successor at TV Today. I called him one Sunday seeking an appointment, and without realizing his busy schedule, started telling him about myself and my reasons for wanting to meet him. Without taking any interest in my story he asked me to meet him at 4pm on Wednesday.

As I have narrated earlier, I prepared all my documents and rushed a full hour early to the *Aaj Tak* office, at that time in the Inner Circle in Connaught Place. Monika was the receptionist at TV Today. I waited for quite some time, and then his secretary Shashi directed me to a huge office where a bearded man was sitting, speaking on the phone with a relative, perhaps his Mama. I took a seat and raised my hands to rub my sweating face.

His shrewd eyes instantly noticed and captured my wristwatch. "Ghadi Badi Mehangi Hai," he said.

"Sir, gift me mili hai," was all that I could reply, without revealing the fact that it was worth a mere hundred rupees, purchased from the Connaught Place market.

We conversed for twenty minutes and then he directed me to Waheed Naqvi, his deputy at *Aaj Tak*. Midway through talking to Naqvi, I noticed Deepak Chaurasia shouting at one of his copywriters. Waheed Naqvi did not take more than a minute to reject me – I was quite unexperienced and was still to finish my study course, which he had already understood.

I had no words to describe my psychological state. The earth and sky were spinning before my eyes. I took a round of the Inner Circle in that state of mind and bought a cold drink to relax my mind. This was normal practice for me for the series of rejections I faced in the media industry.

After that, I must have made about two dozen phone calls to Rahul Dev. One time he came to the phone and agreed to give me an appointment. But I never disclosed why I could not join him, or what Waheed Naqvi had said to me.

I have no regrets or complaints for either, Rahul Dev or Waheed Naqvi. Three to four years later when Sanjaya Pugalia took over from Rahul Dev, I met him also, but then he was moving to Mumbai to start a new venture.

South Campus had been my shelter and headquarters upon returning from each interview. I came back to the nice surroundings to meet my friends and to have lunch at Murthy's canteen. That is how we all – Sarvada, Vikram, Brajesh, Manish,Vashistha and CK spent our days in South Campus.

And in between this team of Fukray(Delhi's lingo used for those teenagers who does not have to do anything) people,one fine day when I returned to South Campus I saw a bunch of girls near Murthy's canteen newly admitted in a management course in South Campus. My eyes stucked on a little dark and tall girl who was sipping a cup of tea along with her friends in beautifully designed cup which perhaps she had brought from her house in to Girls Hostel.It gave me a thunderbolt almost in same way as the Michael Carleone of "The Godfather" had got when he saw her future counter part in Sicily,Italy. Perhaps she gave me lope sided smile and that was enough to forget all my worries.I fell in love with this attractive,little dark and tall girl then and there and firmly thought that I will go ahead to meet her after knowing her details.Those were hard days for all of us, and I will never forget South Campus, and how it sheltered us all and that beautiful,little dark and tall girl who still comes in my dream even after 18 years,with whom I got to meet and express my feelings,how ever I do not know if she ever felt same way as I did.

My journey, which began in Lucknow, was taking a tough turn, but I was determined like a rock that I would make it – whatever it took.

And destiny was awaiting me at the BBC, and Madhukar Upadhyaya finally promised me an internship there.

This was the time when India was experiencing the satellite television revolution. There were only couple of channels; Zee, NDTV-Star, Jain and TVI. The BBC by that time had shut down its half an hour show on Home TV.

The journey was tough, but so was the traveller.

This was the summer of 1998. The story was unfolding and so were the wings of time for the Indian news industry.

fancycrave/Pexels photo

Into the Magical Realm of the BBC

By the time I contacted the BBC Delhi office for my internship, Mr Madhukar Upadhyaya had left for London. But I went up to the BBC office, and Swati, who was handing production at that time, asked me to wait perhaps making a phone call to London. Impatient, I waited until she returned and thanked God that Mr Upadhyaya had verified my claims.

I was asked to meet Seema Chishti, then Bureau Chief of the Hindi Service. I had already listened to her husky voice many times on the BBC Radio programmes so it was a a pleasure to speak to her. I rang her up and she asked me to meet het the next day. Again, as mentioned I gathered up my certificates and reached the BBC's 1-Rafi Marg office. It was a Sunday and no one else was in the office. Seema went over all my certificates, which I felt was not really required. Then she allowed asked me to start my internship the next day.

It was an exceptional opportunity. The BBC does not have a provision for interns, instead allowing traineeship at its HQ in London. But for me it was an opportunity and I was eager to grab it. We all know that the BBC is known for its Radio Services, and that the TV services of the BBC came much latter. It started its first broadcast in India in 1932, with the inception of the BBC Hindustani Service. After partition it was bifurcated into the BBC Hindi and Urdu Service.

Since then the BBC's radio broadcasts have created waves across mostly rural (mostly) India. The broadcasts during the 1971 war, Indira Gandhi's assassination and General Elections, in India were some of the events in history through which the BBC firmly established its charisma in the Indian subcontinent.

I can narrate a story about the reliability of the BBC. The late Prime Minister Mr Rajiv Gandhi was in Calcutta at the moment when Indira Gandhi was assassinated. He got to know about it, but did not trust the information and kept a radio set stuck next to him throughout the flight back to Delhi, only believing the news when the BBC announced the tragedy.

The BBC has also been home to some of the prominent figures who served within, like Balraj Sahni, Inder Kumar Gujral, Purushottam Lal Pahwa, Onkar Nath Srivastava and Kailash Budhwar.

© Shutterstock / Claudio Divizia

Not to say that the BBC is considered to be a trusted name, but somehow in recent years it has lost its charisma among its popular listeners.

During my internship I got to work with Seema Chishti, a St Stephens graduate, Mike Woodridge, who was heading the South-Asia bureau, Salma Zaidi, as well as Shalini Joshi, who was a new face in the BBC at that time.

However, I most keenly observed Andrew Whitehead and Satish Jacob, who were working on a series of stories at the BBC. Satish Jacob was a really humble man who, who along with Mark Tully, wrote the book on Indira Gandhi's assassination.

India was celebrating its first fifty years of independence in 1998 and every producer in the BBC was preparing a special program to mark the day. I felt a huge amount of pride on this special occasion which left an unforgettable mark on me. However, I was unable to understand the behaviour of the two ladies who asked me that day to wind up my internship the very next day. Perhaps, I was involved more than I was required or maybe it was felt that I had learnt quite enough from the BBC.

Whatever the reason, the two ladies called me into a cabin and said let's stop my internship. I asked for the reason as there were still four days left in my internship period. They said nothing but for me to leave.

I was shocked and tried to call London to speak to Mr Madhukar Upadhyaya, but I now feel that he was not consulted about the decision.

I thanked Seema Chishti for releasing all my certificates immediately and for helping me learn about so many new things, and returned back to South Campus.

The BBC, by that time, had made me learn about the ABC's of journalism.

It was my first brush with an international organisation, at the age of 22. I ended my relationship with the BBC in August 1998 but to this day I remain in touch with its people there.

My days in Zee News (Zee India TV)

Again I was out of an internship. The only consolation point I had was that I was still continuing with my studies, but felt that I would not stop. I gathered all my courage, tried to wipe out away my tears and hurt from the BBC experience, and rang up my only sympathisers in the BBC – Madhukar Upadhyaya and Shalini Joshi. Since Madhukar was away from my reach, I relied on Shalini Joshi, a relatively new face at the BBC. She immediately answered my call and asked me to go and meet Mr Shiv Prasad Joshi, one of the most reliable recognizable faces in Zee India TV (now Zee News).

With no other option left, I put my trust in her words and soon got an time appointment with Mr Joshi. I was very keen to see the budding new face of the Indian news industry. To remind my readers, there were only three channels in the Indian TV news circuit at that time – Zee India TV, Aaj Tak and NDTV -Star News.

I do not remember how I managed to get inside the Zee News Corporation, but Shiv Joshi eventually played a major role in helping me learn about the scripting side of things. A rather young and energetic bearded man with sharp skills of packaging and narration, he was a prominent and most highly reliable face of Zee India TV.

It was October 1998 when I began working in Zee India TV's two room office. I was still staying in Mahipalpur and slowly picking up the local Jat lingo. My duty working hours were mostly the night shifts as most interns were relegated to time periods to learn when there was no great news load. My routine was to come to South Campus first and then to take the number 323 bus direct to Nodia Gole Chakkar, and then a rickshaw to Film City. By that time Zee India TV had shifted its office to Film City in Noida, and had taken on its present logo of Zee News.

Not to say that Zee News is a mecca for beginners and learners, but you do get plenty of opportunities to learn new skills on a professional and personal front.

I was put on the newsdesk working mostly under Shiv Joshi's leadership. The Hindi and English news team would work in the same news room, and there was no demarcation among work and people.

This was at a time in Zee News when everyone, from the editor-in-chief to the interns, were all trying to put in their best efforts – their 100%. The regular employees were aiming to get promoted and the interns to secure a foothold in the only Hindi-English news channel running 24-7. Rakesh Khar, our editor in chief, was a humble man with a sharp instinct on who to pick for what work. He nurtured many new faces during that time, many of whom are now big shots in the Indian TV Industry.

And yes, right there in between was I, an intern who had come all the way from a small religiously warm and disputed town, living under the shadow of the Babri Masjid demolition and its consequences. Throughout my early days, I had never been able to forget the faces of the several Hindu and Muslim families who had lost their lives in the Battle of Babri. This was the one issue that had pushed me to choose a career in the news, over a more comfortable one in the field of science. God knows I never liked discussing this issue, and sometimes was even reluctant to tell the people at Zee News that I was from Ayodhya. Most people who wanted to know more would be very curious about all that had happened there in the past.

So my daily routine started at 3:00pm each day. I would come into the office, take some footage from reporters or from the news wire, and then log it on the preview machine. This was the place where I noticed that some of the time I had the company of a beautiful girl sitting next to me on another machine. It was an interesting job that involved rolling the machine backward and forward to see all the footage, and then to note down the counters on it.

My job was to return the tape with the counters to the person in charge and then it was his decision to select whom he wanted to give the tape to for writing the script. I was always dying to write the scripts and doi the voice-overs. There was one shift in charge who knew my eagerness, but always pushed me back onto the preview machine to do more logging, which I hated. I just wanted to write the scripts and do the voice-overs.

And Shiv Joshi knew this. I was always a pleasant person, and if Shiv were the shift-in charge on any day, that day I would get to write at least four scripts and record two voice-overs.

Almost a month later I realized that the beautiful girl sitting on the next preview machine was actually an intern and was studying for a course in DCAC.

So eventually, my hunt for more scripts and more voice-overs was finally fulfilled when our editor-in-chief put me in charge of the night shift on a permanent basis.

The night shift involved more fun and less work for all of us, and while working there the day came that changed my inner being forever.

Walkie-talkies were used primarily for guest coordination on those days and also to for coordination between the late night pick-ups and drops. It was an unusually cold night with pouring rain in the chilling winter of December in Delhi. My pick-up van had reached the office and we were just getting ready to start our shift, which involved sorting out stories from outstation bureaus, desk and wires.

My shift in-charge was holding a walkie-talkie to check who else had left on that rainy night. All of a sudden a female voice crackled over the walkie-talkie, "My pick-up car has crashed at Ashram, I am unable to reach the office in time." And then voice broke out and vanished from the small device. We tried to figure out who it was, and started leaving messages for other vehicles along that route. However, even after an hour we did had not received any message from that unknown female voice.

Then someone banged on the doors of the news-room. The lady who entered was half drenched, dressed in a yellow t-shirt and blue jeans, and was almost smiling at her victory over the weather, as she had managed to reach the office well in time. She was the one person who later managed to prevent the only English bulletin of Zee News from being shut down. I must admit that it was a day which would have been shaky for all of us, if the English team had not arrived in time, as later we got to know that it was the first trial run of the English bulletin, which was to be closely watched by Subhash Chandra.

That daring lady is now at a very senior position serving passionately within the world's biggest news agency.

I learnt that day how to manage the risks and dangers involved during crucial operations of news channels.

We were a small team of interns, producers, reporters and desk personnel, but that very team steered the path for Zee News to achieve the glory of today. Perhaps no one from that team is still working for Zee News, but the mark made by them and the effort put in by us all is still remembered by everyone today, most having moved on to higher places in the media industry.

Now that the English bulletin service on Zee News has been wrapped up, each member of that team, the full time employees as well as interns, both have a deep sense of pride, along with all good wishes for the leading lady who dared to survive and saved us all and the bulletin on that chilling day.

.

Igor Ovsyannykov photo

Our Bureau Chief and Rajdeep Sardesai

Our Bureau Chief at Zee News was Satish K. Singh, a man who always liked field reporting and who was always pushing young blood reporters to go into the field and experience the nitty-gritty of how reporting takes shape. Many believed that he was a confused person, forever trying to resolve the balance between reporting and desk-work. But, to date, I believe that he was a man of merit who deserved a great deal but was pushed back by his rivals in Zee News. However, I always admired about him and appreciated how he carried me along to assist him in some of his brilliant reports he filed during the beginning phase of coalition politics in India.

He did however have a childish habit of biting his nails whenever he was tense with his reports. A man hailing from Bihar, he had possessed a strong team bonding capacity with him. I am most grateful to him for the moment when he brought me to have a face-to face meeting with today's magnet of Indian news television – Rajdeep Sardesai.

I had finished my night shift and was planning to go back to my one room accommodation in Mahipalpur, when I saw my bureau chief looking tense and indulged in his old habit of nail biting. He asked me whether I wanted to accompany him to an interview with Madhavrao Scindia at his residence. There was a political crisis in a remote North Eastern region, and the chief minister had submitted his resignation directly to Congress supremo, Sonia Gandhi.

I was falling asleep but said that I would go along with him, not knowing for certain what would come from it.

Rajdeep Sardesai, then political editor, (it was perhaps November 1998), of NDTV-Star News, was already a charismatic and media mobilizer, a famous name and is still serving the Indian television industry with the same passion and energy that has become his USP among his fellow workers and Indian viewers.

This was the promise. The desire to meet him was the reason which made me decide to accompany my bureau chief, even after a hectic and tiring night shift.

When we reached Madhavrao Scindia's residence a couple of television journalists were already there waiting for him to come out. All of sudden a car with the NDTV-Star News logo entered the premises, the two men who stepped out of the car being the famous duo of Rajdeep and Arnab. We held our breath as the stage was set. Tea was served to us all in beautifuly designed cups and plates, and together we were still waiting for Madhavrao Scindia to come out.

Rajdeep was prepared as he asked for a link from his studio. Patting on his notebook, his brain was kept busy designing some grilling questions, while Arnab kept pacing alongside the office van.

And then my bureau chief whispered in my ear; "Scindia ji." I woke from my stupor and realized that the gun mikes and lights were focused straight on Madhavarao Scindia. Links had been restored and the great interviewer of Indian media had just thrown a chilling question to Mahadaji.

Later, I spoke to with Rajdeep and he asked me to meet him in his office. Right from that moment on I have met him on several occasions, both officially and personally. The last has been thirteen good years ago and the newshound has sharpened his skills of grilling the interviewees, but has grown into a more humble and patient listener since then also... so I have been told by my friends.

He has brought in the first international collaboration in Indian television news and has set up a team of passionate reporters and producers who have changed the destiny of television news, but for me he is still the same person whom I saw at Madhavrao Scindia's residence, and who always picks up my phone without ever making me wait.

Campaign Trail

Elections in India are like mega festivals. They are as national, colourful, bright, and sweet and sour as are Holi, Diwali and Eid. Right from the country's first general elections they have been organised and conducted with the efforts of all officially involved and unofficially participating people, on such a large scale that observers come from outside India to witness this political extravaganza.

One can see a wave of enthusiasm and energy among all those who are a part of this largest democracy in the world. Children, young and old see it as an opportunity to use their might through the people who have the right to vote and elect their respective leaders. And so, in India, this festival is conducted and celebrated in a different mood altogether.

I remember when I was a child we were all very enthusiastic about the banners and posters that were circulated amongst people during the elections. We used a few of them as cover pages for our books and some to show our affection for our candidates from the area. Posters and banners have often changed the mood of elections at times. And if I am not mistaken, in one incident I remember when the posters of the last speech made by Indira Gandhi changed the fortunes of the candidates in the 1984 General Elections.

But now I refer to the elections of 1999. It had been seven years since the demolition of the Babri Mosque, and India's nationalist Hinduist party had been able to create a wave of nationalism and Hindu mass movement across the nation. They and had managed to gain partial success in the elections in terms of number of seats in parliament. The Congress party was suffering a big huge setback in previous elections and India had just entered an era of coalition politics, where no party was untouchable to another. Coalition politics had earlier been practised at the center level and we were now heading towards another such phase of it in the 1999 elections.

Our team at Zee News was working very hard to prepare itself for the election coverage, and we were feeling the heat of Hinduistic nationalistic feeling, there being slightly less of an option for Congress to win a majority in the election, the channel designing an optimistic program called the 'Campaign Trail'.

But I was feeling a differently way, and am not talking about the election results. My feelings may or may not be in favor of any particular political party, but my concern was that the base on which this Hindu mass movement was created was creating a vacuum which has a disastrous impact on society's role in challenging the basic ethos of a strong base of a secular democracy. But the vacuum was there and no one was trying to realise it. And I too became a part of this program of Zee News, which would later become the USP of general elections on Indian Television.

The idea behind the program was that a team of reporters and producers would spend 24 hours with a respected political candidate and would picture it as one single episode. It was a huge exercise and two different centers were created for this show in which a dozen of producers, reporters and script writers had to work together to design the program.

It was the second phase of my internship which provided me with a chance to see the people I respected. I was in team A and it was during the second week of my internship when I noticed that a fresh group of interns had just arrived from the Symbiosis Institute. Three of the interns were put in team A.

We worked very hard in this team. For a period of one month we were detached from the main news team, where we prepared a total of 13 episodes, out of which all thirteen candidates picturised by us won the elections. The three interns from symbiosis really did put in a fabulous effort, and we all were very appreciated for our efforts.

Despite our best efforts and the fact that we often worked in double shifts and handled most of the routine jobs at Zee News, a large number of interns were asked to leave after the election results. I was one of them. It was perhaps a tragedy for us all whose names were broadly written in big black letters on the list which was pasted right in front of the Input room. All the interns unitedly accepted this with a lot of courage since we realized that the only single news channel in India was unable to accommodate almost twenty interns. But there were a lucky few who were selected to stay back and were promoted as trainees.

Everybody, from my team mates to the bureau chief, were sure that keeping in mind my long association and hard work with Zee News, I would be promoted to join the main news team as usual. But sadly after two years of hard work I discovered through the same group of interns who stood back, that the man behind my exit was none other than the same shift in charge who also happened to be my in charge team leader on the campaign trail.

I accepted my exit, and by God's grace there was someone there to support me financially. My elder brother had resigned from BITS Pilani and had joined an MNC in Noida. Hence, I had the time to put my energy into searching for a job. I searched not knowing that it was going to be big, hectic and depressing battle for me.

And then I started using all my contacts and all the promises made to me by all the biggies in the media to get a foothold in the industry; a second entry into a television channel.

I was sure there was something waiting for me out there – something useful, more creative and interesting which would fall my way. But this big gap of joblessness then gave me the positive energy to develop some important contacts and I used my savings to stand on my own as an independent journalist who uncovered some of the evils in society thorough unrecognised reports which I dispatched to some of the best people and organizations.

In the meantime I took few an Electronic News Gathering class at film school but primarily utilized this phase of joblessness to gather my head on my broken shoulders and stood as one. I was then recognised by a person to an individual whom I still admire.

Although I had never worked with her, she helped by providing me with the contact of the most powerful person on this planet.

Anita Pratap never knew me; who I was and what I did; but she trusted me. She had just left CNN as its South Asia bureau chief. I had never met her, but her emails gave me the courage to sharpen my skills of dispatching reports. To this date she has continued to email me even when she is in Norway and is on diplomatic assignments.

I have no words to thank her for the skills and courage she instilled in me on how to file email dispatches from crisis zones, which were later sent to many organizations and individuals to which I assay the most lengthy and unrecognised work in media.

Doing such work and using most of my time at home I learnt much and made the kind of contacts that have been useful my entire life. Then came the year which was a rather fruitful one for me. And I can bet that what I learnt and the kind of contacts I developed after that year now carry more weight over my entire life.

2002 AD and Two Ladies

Anita Pratap bears the credit of being the first woman to head CNN in South Asia. This lady from Kerla is the first international journalist to interview the LTTE chief, deep in Jafna during his heyday. She has been internationally recognized and awarded for her journalistic assignments during her days at CNN and Time Magazine.

It is a little uncomfortable to write about Anita Pratap as the entire Indian and international media knows about the challenging assignments she undertook during her reporting days. Upon her resignation from CNN she married the Norwegian Ambassador to India, and shuttled between Norway and India, pursuing diplomatic assignments and helping her husband.

Quite often she visits India to make some documentaries and to meet her extended family here.

One day when I was trying to see who I could could approach to rely on for help I came upon her number and called her. She immediately picked the phone up and spoke to me. Then we started exchanging emails, and every time I mailed her regarding elaborating some problem or difficulty, she would come up with a solution for it. However I have never met her, but her emails are almost like a face-to-face meeting, and I always turn to her whenever I am in need or require her advice.

We have shared comments on her books, on her ongoing assignments and also a little about future plans. She never forgets to wish me well whenever I achieve anything remarkable in my professional as well as personal life.

We continue to share ideas and this was during the 2003 U.S. led strike on Iraq over the issue of WMDs that she started a signature campaign on the U.S.'s decision to attack Iraq. I also wrote a piece in this campaign. The report was then dispatched to the senior administration in of the U.S. government. And that is how I got to know about the senior administration of President Bush and gained contact with the White House.

Ami Vitale is an internationally acclaimed photojournalist currently based in Florida, U.S.A. She is on the board of selectors for National Geographic magazine – the world famous environment, science and wildlife publication. But she has already so much to her credit, having received numerous awards from international organizations, and has travelled extensively to the remotest parts of the world that her assignments tell her story to the full.

She has been in India for several years covering stories for world famous Getty Images and has told the story of Kashmir, the Gujarat riots, the Ayodhya issue, festivals, fairs, poverty and child issues through her lense.

She is a master storyteller and her pictures make you think twice on the subjects she raises.

The year 2004 had just begun and I was still looking for an assignment to come my way. I was eager to fill this large gap of joblessness and my optimism was soon going to be realized by these two highly acclaimed individuals.

In Rama's Land and Ami Vitale

I was spending my time tracking news on TV channels, watching hopefully for something worthwhile to come out of it for me. It was towards the end of February that news started picking up momentum from Ayodhya. The age old dispute was getting a picked up by news channels, but this time due to an extended chapter of the issue.

One of the main parties from the Hindu side was going to organise an event which they called Ram Shila Pujan. This event was to be organised to show the commitment of the Hindus to build a glorious Ram Temple on the site of the birthplace of their holy God, Ram.

Now to remind my readers a little about the issue and Ayodhya, I do not wish to repeat the same old story of 1990 and 1992, but would like to add that Ayodhya is one of the oldest cities in Hindu mythology. Situated on the banks of the mighty river Saryu, it is believed that the city was built by Hindu's law giver and the first human being on earth – Manu or rather 'Swayambhu Manu', as he is called. As the Sanskrit verse states:-

Koslo Naam Muditah

Sfeeto Janpado Mahan

Nivishtah Saryu Teere

Prabhuto Dhan Dhanyavaan

Ayodhya Naam Nagri

Tatrshollok Vishrutah

Manuna Manvendrena

Ya Puri Nirmita Swyam.

The lineage of Suryavanshi Kshatriya which started with the Ikshvaku, the remote ancestors of Lord Rama, starts from Ayodhya which was known as Kosla. During the Mahajanpada period Ayodhya, Kosla was one of the sixteen mighty kingdoms in India.

Lorda Rama was the son of Dashratha and the eldest of four sons. He, according to Hindu mythology, is also considered the seventh incarnation of Lord Vishnu.

Now the story is that Shakari Vikrmaditya of the Gupta dynasty built a magnificent Ram temple in Ayodhya which was preserved, refurnished and redecorated by other Hindu kings over time. It is believed that Babar, the first Moughal emperor ordered his aid Mir Baaki to destroy this Ram temple, and subsequently to build a mosque over there.

The people of Ayodhya, along with a section of historians, also believe that the mosque, which was destroyed by an unstructured unorganised mob gathered on the call of Hindu hardliner leaders in 1992, was the same mosque, to which Hindus believe was built after the demolition of the Ram Temple.

Now it has become a matter of dispute between Hindus and Muslims, and the battle has been fought in and outside Indian courts for the last sixty years.

First there was a monk who first filed a petition claiming that the land and structure that belongs to the Hindus in the 1940's is now no more. Ramchandra Paramhans, a Hindu hardliner leader and monk in Ayodhya decided to call Hindus to strengthen their unity and to lay claim on the Ram temple in 2004. And the event to be later organized, was called Ram Shila Pujan.

Present day Ayodhya is a place of Hindu pilgrimage place and is situated 125 kms east of the state capital, Lucknow. It is an assembly constituency seat and is a part of Faizabad district, a once glorious centre of the Nawab of Awadh. It is believed that there are almost 3,000 temples in Ayodhya of which a chain of temples are located on the banks of the holy river Saryu.

It is a small town surrounding which is a populous agricultural land region on the southern side banks of the Saryu making the area productive and the people to mostly dependant on this agricultural business. Some noted Samajwadi and Congress party leaders also have their lineage from this area.

The twin towns of Ayodhya and Faizabad, both of which are parted by a distance of hardly five kilometers, are clear evidence of Hindu-Muslim unity, or as its referred to, Ganga Jamuni tehjeeb.

But the dispute of the Ram Mandir/Babri Mosque has widened the gap between these two communities, and after 1992 when the Babri mosque was demolished, the bitterness had increased tremendously.

On providing the backdrop of this, Hindu hardliners decided to organise the event of Ram Shila Pujan, this story started taking shape in the form of headlines on TV channels towards the end of February 2003.

I, who was looking to jump on such an opportunity, decided to go to Ayodhya and file the my reports to the best people and organizations, who still refused to recognise the situation.

When I entered Ayodhya I felt the heat of tension, security vigilance and also the gathering of dozens of print and TV journalists scattered in lodges and hotels of the twin town. Ayodhya happens to be my birthplace and home town, hence I decided to rest there for the first few days. On this occaison I utilized the time to study the mood of the people and the city and at a glance realized that it was going to be a few eventful weeks.

Some TV teams stationed themselves on the banks of the Saryu, while some had set up their OB vans in the middle of the town. I took a few rounds of the city, talked to people, and visited all possible places in the next couple of days. The colour saffron was the in-thing all over town and Hindu hardliners were busy giving fiery statements in support of the event that they scheduled in for the first week of March.

The disputed area is located in the heart of the city, around which is a three-layered security barricade. It covers an area of roughly 70 acres, on the western side of which stood the disputed structure, until December 6, 1992. You have to go inside the security zone up to about two kilometers before you finally reach the site of Ram Lala.

The monk who organised the event was also a religious leader belonging to the Digamabar Akhara, one of seven Akharas in Ayodhya which manages various temples. His mass is three kilometers from the disputed site and close to the workshops where stones are being shaped for temple construction.

One fine morning I went to my uncle's house in the heart of town to seek some medicine, since he is a homeopathic doctor and was just sitting there sipping a cup of tea. The precursor of the event had started taking shape, and newsmen were busy picturing the places and people around town. All of a sudden a red Maruti car came and stopped in front of my uncle's house and a lady came out with a driver to get herself adjusted in this religiously warm town. I noticed that there was some dispute between the driver and the lady over the exchange of money, perhaps, the hired driver was charging double the amount from a photojournalist who had come all the way from Delhi to cover the event. It was only after my uncle and I intervened that the matter was sorted out, and the lady introduced herself to my homeopathic doctor uncle as Ami Vitale, a journalist from Delhi.

Ami Vitale, as I later discovered was a photojournalist hired by Getty Images, who had already covered events in Kashmir and Gujrat.

At this point I also dared to introduce myself and my plans. She immediately said that she wanted a person to assist her to cover the events that were supposed to unfold in the next couple of weeks. I, all impressed with her intelligence and eagerness, agreed to be in her company until her departure from the town. Of course, we negotiated the terms and conditions before we started our two weeks journey together.

The next morning she called me and said she would pick me up at 6:00am sharp from my uncle's residence. I was not sure what she was going to do at such an early hour. It would have been unwise to go back to my village and come back at 6:00am the next morning, hence I decided to stay at a place that was close to the disputed site. Aurobindo Ashram, a branch of Auroville ashram in Pondicherry, is a small meditation center in Ayodhya, with which I had been associated since I was in class ten. There is a small guest-house located in the serene atmosphere of Aurobindo Ashram, where I stayed to meet Ami until the next morning.

I could not sleep that night as was restless about this new assignment. So, without getting any sleep I reached the meeting point almost half an hour in early, and sat sipping a cup of tea in a stall as my uncle's house was locked at such a time and waited for Ami to arrive.

Sharp at 6:00am, the same red Maruti car stopped in front of my uncle's house and I rushed towards it to see if everything was okay.

She was a little tense, but waved at me and asked me to get into her small car. Upon reaching the river bank, just above the bridge we realised that the sun was about to rise. We left the car and headed towards the eastern bank. We must have walked for about half a mile and saw small pyres burning on the riverbank. It was the place for performing the last rites of the Hindus. I stopped Ami and told her that it might be unwise to head towards that side, as it would give us a pleasant feeling. So, we returned and started walking alongside the river. Ami, as a sharp photo journalist took out her ultra modern long range camera and lens and took up a position by wading two meters into the Saryu river. She took a couple of shots of the bridge and then of people who were taking a bath in the river. It is considered a holy feeling to take a bath early in the morning in the river according to Hindu mythology. I was standing on the riverside steps as I saw she was waving her hand and calling me towards her. She was willing to learn about the river, and the ghats and about the Sadhus who were busy doing their meditation on the riverbank. I told her that it is was considered important to meditate and take a bath early in the morning in a holy river, according to Hindu mythology. Then she took a few shots of the rising sun. The sun was just appearing from over the backyards of long distant planes of the river bank, just above the surface of the river.

She tried to move a little deeper into the river, as I admired her expertise with the camera. She remained static standing in the deep chilling water of the river for more than half an hour and took continuous shots of the rising sun.

We had finished our task on the eastern side of the river bank, and now headed to the bridge to cross it and move towards the western bank. Most of the temples are lined up alongside the river, and a small stream out from the Saryu has been metamorphosed into the 'Ram Ki Paudi'. The real event was awaiting us on that side as we moved towards the bridge.

The woman, who was breastfeeding her son and the school which that was abandoned.

As soon as we headed towards the western side of the river we saw a small mob carrying saffron flags in their hands, moving just over the bridge. They were shouting slogans in support of Ram Janm Bhumi. We avoided the mat and reached moved towards the line of temples alongside the small stream called 'Ram ki Paudi'.

Ami was determined to enter the temples and take some photographs. There is a very famous Shiva Temple which is known as Nageshwar Nath. We decided to enter and soon discovered that Ami had climbed up on the rooftop somehow after having a chat with the Pujari of the temple. I followed her and moving along narrow, dark stairs I too soon found myself on the rooftop.

The sun had emerged above the surface of the river and its rays were touching and entering the curls of the water waves. Ami took hundreds of photographs of the river, the rising sun, the temple bylanes and the houses alongside the ghats.

This was the time when most of the temples had started the 'Subah ki Aarti' (worshiping the lords Gods and making him awake theme). We participated in the 'Subah ki Aarti' and then sat down on the bank for a while to plan our next course of action.

Ami was insisting that we get inside some houses and talk with the members of families to get a clearer idea on what exactly they thought of the Ram Temple issue. I was not so sure about going into people's houses at such an early stage of the day.

But then, we ended up deciding to get into atl east a couple of houses, or rather homes built inside the houses inside the temples.

We selected one rather small temple in which a family of six people were living – a man, his wife and their two sons, one daughter and a newborn. We talked to them and soon realised they were not interested in any kind of debate about the Ram Temple issue, as they believed there could be no argument about the fact that Ram was born in Ayodhya and that the whole place belonged to the Hindus. As we were talking to the man Ami went inside the house and perhaps tried to talk to the mother of the newborn baby. As I got to know later, the mother was breastfeeding her newborn son and Ami had insisted on taking their photos of mother breastfeeding.

By now It was 7:30am, and we had to go back to our places to freshen up, and then to get back to work again and head for our destinations.

At 10:00am we met at a restaurant and chalked out the plan for the whole day. We decided to see the bylanes and temples first, and then visit the nearby areas in search of meeting and talking to the people and residents of Ayodhya.

Ayodhya city stretches along both sides of the National Highway which connects the state capital Lucknow with another important city – Gorakhpur. On regular intersections this highway is divided by narrow roads which allow you to enter the temple town from the western side of the road, while the majority of the residents and houses are located on the eastern side of the road. There is a very odd distribution of temples and common residents in Ayodhya. These narrow bylanes take you to various temples right from the entrance of Ayodhya to the extreme north of the town where the river Saryu flows eastward.

We decided to pick the west side of the road to enter the temple bylanes. The road which connects the national highway goes deep into the temple bylanes, touching most of the important temples, including the disputed site.

These bylanes are occupied by small shops selling sweets, idols, sandals, Khandaukhandau (wooden Chappalsslippers), books of rituals, Kanthikanthi-Malamala (Holy necklaces) and other useful items; goods you generally required in traditional Hindu rituals.

The most interesting thing is that in the bylane which connects the National Highway to the disputed site, you will see the CDs, DVDs and cassette recordings of the 1992 demolition event of the mosque and speeches of Hindu hardliner leaders.

The first temple you see is called Hanuman Garhi. It is a prominent temple where the idols of Hanuman, along with those of his mother Anjana, attract your attention from a distance. You have to after crossing about 75 odd steps before you reach the temple. Naga Sadhus manage the whole temple area. This is done by dividing the whole area of the temple into seven pattis (divisions). Each patti is owned an Akhara akhara and is where wrestlers are groomed.

We crossed Hanuman Garhi and Kanak Bhavan (House of Gold), and proceeded towards a narrow lane which connects with a small Muslim area, and further crosses to a Jain temple on the west side and another temple bylane on the north side. Towards the south of this small narrow area is again another cluster of temples. At a glance no one can fail to notice this tiny area, comprising of perhaps a dozen or so houses or even less.

Ami was determined to get inside this area. I too agreed but advised her to come with me and meet a very calm and intellectual person who had lived in a lonely house situated alongside this area.

Ami agreed and we headed forward to meet Dr R.C .Prasad.

Dr R.C. Prasad was an intelligent and knowledgeable person who had a lot of information having an extreme knowledge about the town and its problems. A very humble man, he had moved from Agra along with his family. However, now he was spending his days all alone. We went to meet him and seek his version of local events.

He was known to me and I was sure that he would be glad to meet with a journalist at his house. He asked us to sit and offered us a chair and a glass of water. He did not speak much but took us inside his beautifully designed house and showed us some trunks, pieces of luggage and kitchenware. I was not sure what he was trying to tell us, until he told us both that the trunks and luggage belonged to some Muslim families who had left town before the event of Ram Shila Pujan out of fear of riots breaking.

Ami took some photographs, but we were both unsure how to react in this situation. Then Dr Prasad told us that even he was planning to leave town.

We thanked Dr Prasad and headed towards that area we had noticed. I did not find it hard to believe that most of the houses were locked and that families had already left town in order to protect their women and children.

There was no one in this area with whom we could talk to. As soon as we were moving out of the place, we saw a small structure standing in ruins. At first we could not identify it, but then I read on the walls of the ruined building; 'Kanya Primary Pathshala' (Girls Primary School).

We could not comprehend whether the school was ruined as a result of the riots that broke out in 1993 after the demolition of the mosque, or if it was really just an old structure that had collapsed due to bad weather.

The sun was moving rapidly moving towards the western sky, we were hungry and had spent the whole day roaming around the town, so we decided to head back towards our destination.

Flag March and Ram Shila Pujan on the Streets of Ayodhya

We spent that night at our respective places while I kept worrying about Ami as the town grew dark. Security was tight across the Faizabad district and Article 144 had been imposed over the whole state of Uttar Pradesh. We were not sure how the day was set to begin, so kept our mobile devices phones on, charged and ready to be received throughout the night.

Media personnel occupied all the lodges, hotels and guest-houses as only a couple of days were left for the event 'Ram Shila Pujan'. I had no authority to enter the town as only government officials, police, security personnel and the media were allowed to roam around freely. So the entire night I was busy discovering the route through which I could reach the hotel where Ami was staying. Finally, and successfully I discovered a route through an isolated, rough road, crossing through many villages and that connected at the end with the Faizabad route, to the hotel where Ami was staying.

I took my old bicycle that I rode when I was in class 12th standard and reached the Hotel Shan-E-Awadh to see Ami and assist her. Ami was all awake and waiting for me. She was tense as she got to know that the army and police were going to conduct a Flag March across the entire town in order to build the confidence level of the town residents who were already frightened, tense and disturbed.

Ami was not sure if I would be able to cope with the situation. She deliberately asked me if I was ready. I nodded that I was determined to accompany her through the tight security and in the tense town.

We drove a small red car and headed towards Ayodhya. We could see police and paramilitary forces all around and sailed past the chowk and noticed that each shop was closed and not a single person was on the streets. Only security vehicles were moving in Faizabad towards Ayodhya. We reached Ayodhya and positioned ourselves at a crossroad which connected the highway with the temple bylane – the same road that stretched towards Hanuman Garhi. We were among our fellows with cameras, both still and TV video, media personnel representing Indian and the western media. Some of them had come from Delhi, while some had landed directly from their respective countries. The Sky News team had landed from Beijing to see how the city of Ayodhya, and the entire nation was going to react on to one of the biggest gatherings after 1992.

It was 07:00 am and not a single person was on the streets, houses and shops were closed. Security personnel were deployed on the streets, in bylanes and above rooftops of houses.

We waited for the Flag March to start. And then we saw a police vehicle announcing the route for the March. Ami and I had just finished our conversation as to which place would be suitable to cover the March, and managed to get inside the patrolling vehicles, paramilitary forces and the horses which were part of the convoy.

I must admit that Ami and I were both working like soldiers deployed in a war zone, all ready with our arsenals.

Just then the Flag March headed from the extreme northern part of the town towards the place where we were positioned – a 'Paidal' battalion first, then followed by a motorcade, a horse battalion, another motorcade and then again another Paidal battalion towards the end. Ami was already equipped with her camera and sat down on the road and snapped a couple of hundred photographs in less than fifteen minutes. She was moving faster with her camera than we can type on our keyboards. And then I saw her expertise when she entered like a hurricane, got inside the convoy and began taking photographs. I waited for her as she waved towards me to get on to the rooftops of nearby houses so we may get some excellent photographs. Within a blink of an eye we were on the rooftop of a house, from where we took hundreds of photographs of the Flag March. While we were negotiating the stairs we saw a lonely child crying without anyone around to take care of him. I took him, knocked at a door and handed him over to a neighbour who knew the parents and then rushed to accompany Ami down a bylane. The Flag March headed towards the workshops where the stones for temple construction were shaped.

The moment the Flag March ended, we found that all the media people were rushing to their workstations to file their reports and grab their breakfast which they had avoided due to the March. There was also a press conference by Ramchandra Paramhans at 11:00am. Ami and I soon found that we were left alone at the crossroad which intersected towards Hanuman Garhi.

Ami put her right hand on my shoulder, and I in turn looked into her eyes. Both of us felt that we were hungry and went to grab breakfast together. Ami then managed to tell me the problem and very politely asked if I had a press ID card. All of sudden I realized what she was talking about. The next day was the event of Ram Shila Pujan and it would be quite difficult for anybody to watch or assist the event without a valid press ID.

We headed to our hotel, as we had to return soon for the press conference. While I was thinking how I could manage to get hold of any local press ID, Ami started transmitting the photographs to the Getty Images office in Delhi. At 10:30 am we were in the same red Maruti 800 car, but now something had changed. There was an absence of talk as silence occupied the place between us.

As we reached the workshop (where the stones were being constructed and where the press conference was to take place), we found that the scene was already set. TV and print media personnel had occupied their places and Ramchandra Paramhans was sitting on a 'Takht' (wooden bed), all waiting for the press conference to start. As Ami and I were adjusting to the unbroken silence between us, a cluster of people started cheering up, they said, "Phone aa gaya....phone aa gaya." And Ramchandra Paramhans rushed to an inner room where a phone was kept. Somebody uttered the words, "Advani ji hain," and then two to three cars came into the premises carrying one of the most prominent Hindu hardliner leaders and general secretary of the VHP (Vishwa Hindu Parishad), – Mr Ashok Singhal.

All of sudden I realized the urgent need for a press ID, but it was at this moment that Ami needed me and I was determined to help her. Soon Ramchandra Paramhans emerged from the room and shouted a slogan "Jai Shri Ram...Karyakram kal hoga."

And with this the press conference started during which both the leaders showed their determination to carry out the Ram Shila Pujan, and subsequently to build a magnificent temple at the disputed site.

As soon as the press conference ended we headed back to our hotel. Ami showed me some of the remarkable photographs she had clicked on the banks of the Saryu, in the bylane and the press conference. I was finding it difficult to react as I was busy thinking about the next day's problem.

The day had ended with not so many speculations, but as the sun dropped in the western sky rumours and news both came around, hand in hand. Some Indian TV channels were broadcasting that thousands of 'Kar Sevaks' were entering the twin towns of Ayodhya and Faizabad from nearby villages. Some took this one step further and claimed that the VHP may start the foundation stone ceremony the next day, and that top BJP leaders may join in.

As a sharp photojournalist Ami asked me to remain in touch with the Indian lobby of journalists, and insisted that I not go to my village that night. However, both the good hotels 'Shan-E-Awadh' and 'Krishna' were occupied by national and international media teams and I was unable to find a room for myself.

We were both puzzled and sat in the cafetaria of the hotel until late while chalking out a plan for the next day. Ami was joined by a Spanish photographer friend, Ima Garmendia, who had come from Madrid to cover the event. She stayed in Ami's room at the hotel.

However, the problem of a valid Press ID card was still there. Late at night I contacted a freelance photographer and asked him if he could give me an ID card. He agreed but asked me to pay Rs 500 but within two hours I had a press ID of a two-page tabloid. However, Ami was not satisfied with this.

There was no place in the hotel for me and I felt that it was not needed as most TV journalists of Indian TV channels were awake because of the information that thousands of Kar Sevaks were trying to get into town.

While I was sitting in the reception area, at around 01:00 am, I saw Ami's driver coming towards me. Someone must have told him about my problem, Ami perhaps.

He said that I could stay in his room in the hotel dormitory, and then went to sleep in the car parked car outside the hotel. I was so tired that I could not refuse his humble request and soon fell asleep.

Around 02:30 am I woke again and was feeling the need to see Ami, as was in constant fear of her not being in a good state of mind. I knocked at the room's door, Ima opened it and allowed me to see Ami and then I returned back to my dormitory after asking her to lock the door and then fell asleep again.

I woke around 10:30 am, only to find that all of them had left to cover the event – Ami, Ima and all the print and TV journalists. There was no one in the hotel. I was astonished as to why Ami had not called me, only to find later that she was more worried about *my* safety. Her driver told me this later.

I came down to the cafeteria and found Mr Ramakant Awasthi, the local Bureau Chief of Dainik Jagran there. He had not left as he was filing a breaking news report to his HQ. I told him about my problem and he then asked me to accompany him to the place where the 'Ram Shila Pujan' was scheduled to take place.

Midway through the drive he told me that the state government has not allowed Ramchandra Paramhans and other hardliners to cross the intersection which led towards the disputed site. Rather, it ordered them to perform the Ram Shila Pujan at the residence of Ramchandra Paramhans in the Digambar Akhara.

I have already described the tight security in and around town. Now it was doubled up on the day. Ramakant Awasthi and I headed towards the workshop from where the convoy was supposed to proceed to Digamabar Akhara to perform the Ram Shila Pujan.

Sky News Team and Ami's Departure

The distance between the workshop place and Digambar Akhara was roughly two and half kilometres. But as was we predicted, the streets, bylanes, intersections and rooftops of temples and houses were occupied by more than 5,000 people in this two and half kilometres stretch. Most of them were local residents and a little over a thousand and a half would be the people who had come in from the nearby villages, and who were referred to as 'Kar Sevaks'. Ramakant Awasthi and I reached the workplace which was located by an isolated route road and as we reached there we found there was no place in and around where we could stand or view the 'Havan' (a pre-ritual before the Ram Shila Pujan). We stood and waited outside.

TV media persons, both (domestic and international) had stationed themselves in the places they found most suitable to cover, but mostly they were all ready to accompany the procession. Some of them on hand climbed onto rooftops to get a clearer view of the whole event.

It was almost impossible for me to look out for Ami in this ocean of men, women and Sadhus. I realized that I had lost her. This worried me. Just then I looked towards Ramakant Awasthi who had moved towards the entrance gate and as I followed him I saw a fat man in his forties coming towards me.

Richard, a British media person, had landed from Beijing, along with his small crew representing Sky News. Richard himself was the editor, while Peter, a rather young man was the correspondent, German born Inka Kretchmer being the producer of the team representing Sky News. I must mention that Sky News is a sister company of the media empire created by Rupert Murdoch, of News Corporation. Sky News primarily broadcasts in Europe and its other sister company Fox News broadcasts on the American continent.

The small Sky News team was confused as what to cover and what not to, so Richard asked for a helping hand which I could not refuse. Knowing that maybe I would not be able to meet Ami and that it would be a great learning experience, I agreed. The Sky News team was using the best technology available – a satellite phone, a link with the Beijing studio, as well as a smart and beautiful producer. We all just walked around and searched for a place where we could station our camera. Finally, Richard suggested that we should occupy a rooftop. Since all the temple structures were in a bad shape we decided to get onto a rather good building.

Now we were on the rooftop of an old structure, just across the road and directly in front of the workshop place we could see all that was going on inside but I still could not see Ami and Ima. Richard asked me to explain what was going on inside the workshop place and I explained that the VHP leaders, Ramchandra Paramh Hans and his 500 followers were performing 'Rudra Ashtadhyayai' – a worship offered to Lord Shiva. Thereafter a procession was supposed to move towards the Digamabar Akhara.

Richard started his PTC on the satellite link, "Hail to Shri Ram…,"…….that this is what we could hear across the holy town of Ayodhya'. He completed this in three minutes and soon we saw that the procession had started moving. We wrapped up our equipment and thanked God that all had gone well but all of a sudden we heard a loud bang and a huge hole appeared in the rooftop. The building was collapsing and all we could see was a man who was reporting for an Indian channel, collapsing into a side hole along with the debris. The hole was aone meter in diameter. We helped the Indian reporter come out and landed safely onto the floor of the building and joined the procession.

The VHP members, the Kar Sevaks and many people joined the procession, while the residents of the town occupied the streets and rooftops.

As I joined the procession I could see that an elderly and rigid monk who had challenged the entire government over his commitment to perform Ram Shila Pujan, had a great fan following. The Ram Shila was kept on a wooden chariot, while the VHP leaders like Ashok Singhal and

Ramchandra Pramhans were walking barefoot behind the chariot. The atmosphere was filled with chants of 'Jai Shri Ram', and we were soon crawling amidst a heavy crowd.

All of sudden I saw Ami and could easily judge that she was more than a little tense as she kept herself busy clicking photographs. Inka Kretchmer, who by now was well versed in communicating with me, whispered in my ear, "Oh that American photographer... she is awesome!"

Ramchandra Paramhans by then had trembled and fallen down twice and was sweating while shouting 'Jai Shri Ram'. Ashok Singhal was holding his hand but insisted on being on his own. And somehow by the time we reached the Digamabar Akhara it was a huge mess. Thousands of people covered every inch of the ground. Inka and I stood in the crowd, while Richard and Peter went inside the Akhara to cover the Ram Shila Pujan. Inka offered me a bottle of water as was all we had at that time.

The Ram Shila Pujan lasted for two and half hours amidst a constant fear of a possible lathi charge, yet we somehow had managed to remain static. The moment it finished we heard the Kar Sevaks shouting, "Jai Shri Ram, Ho Gaya Kaam." I saw Richard and Peter coming out and hired a taxi to the Krishna Palace hotel, from where he was supposed to go live for Sky News. I said farewell to the Sky News team at the Krishna Hotel and then rushed to the Shan-E-Awadh to see if I would be able to meet Ami. As soon as I reached "Shan-E-Awadh" I realized, and to my astonishment, Ami and Ima had both left to catch a flight from Lucknow to Delhi.

I was nervous, pained and emotional at this. I had thought that perhaps when I knocked at her hotel room door and Ima opened I would get one last chance to see Ami. I was determined to see her at least once in Delhi, so did not bother to go back to my village, as I had my luggage with me. An Associated Press journalist gave me a ride up to Lucknow and from there I reached Charbaagh Railway Station at 10:00 pm to catch the Lucknow mail.

The next day, early in the morning, I knocked at my brother's residence in Noida.

Ami had left her Delhi address in my uncle's diary, which I had copied into mine. I told my brother that I was going to consult a library in the South Campus, but was actually determined to go to Defense Colony to the address that Ami had left. Perhaps it was just a coincidental meeting with her in Ayodhya, which should not have been prolonged to Delhi, I thought. Ami was staying on the second floor of a beautifully built house. I held my breath as I spoke to the guard. He asked me several questions before finally reflecting my name on a mirror which he showed to Ami over a camera.

I was not sure how Ami would react, but waited for her to come out. The next moment I saw the lady whom I had helped to the best of my efforts. She came out on to the terrace and said, "Go away, leave me alone."

Sometimes you meet people and develop a bond with them, and then all of sudden when the thread of that bonding is broken you feel nothing but start acting like a fool. That was my state of mind when I was coming out onto the main road. I felt as if I had lost all my money and savings in a gamble.

My next destination was the one place that was not untouchable to every single student who had no money to get enrolled into an academic program, but wanted to enjoy a campus life – my own South Campus.

I entered like a hero and felt like a star when someone told me, "Oh I saw you on TV, you were standing behind a monk." I realized that perhaps this was the reward which Ami had saved for me.

And then some one came in my mind.For a short stint I felt that I had done a heroic task in Ayodhya coping with Ami in tough situation but at the same time I was hurt with her behavior in Delhi. I don't know how the little dark and tall girl of South Campus started occupying my mind and I decided to saty little late in South Campus on that very hurtful day. I collected all my wisdom,courage and bravery and went to Geeanjali Hostel(The Only Girl's Residential Hostel in South Campus) and asked security to give a call to the girl who had snatched my sleeps even when I was working with Ami in Ayodhay. To my astonishment she came out.Perhaps Ii expressed my feelings to her,I am sure I had that courage with me. I still do not know what she said but we were destined to meet at several other occasions in near future.

Sardesai Syndrome

As I was trying to understand Ami's behaviour I was also busy talking to my friends about what I did in Ayodhya. Murthi served me a good south Indian lunch and Nagesh, who was the cigarette supplier for South Campus, was there to give me a packet of cigarettes. I somehow overcame the 'Ami factor' and tried to enjoy the atmosphere of South Campus. But I knew that once again I was going to face the same challenges and the same amount of struggles in this new phase where I had to indulge myself in the search for a job.

So I rested in South Campus for a whole day, and then again took the number 323 bus to Noida. My mind was mapping all the possible avenues I could explore for a job in the media industry. This time I was a little confident that my experiences in Ayodhya would help me in finding a place in this industry. My mind explored all possible TV Channels, and also this time as well as, international media organizations I was intending to explore.

I reached my brother's residence and without discussing anything with my parents, (who had already arrived from Ayodhya to join the rest of us) and my brother I went to sleep. I started writing down all the addresses and contact numbers which I was planning to try the next day in a diary and as I was addicted, first rang up the BBC office around 11:00 clock the next day. Just to remind all of you and I do not know why but I had started writing e-mail dispatches, the inspiration for which I had got from Anita Pratap, about whatever I had observed in Ayodhya. I filed e-mail reports to big shots in the media industry, like Rajdeep Sardesai and also to people in the BBC. I do not know whether it was the pressure of joblessness or my cynical desire to be a journalist, but I dispatched all my e-mails to the BBC HQ in London, addressed to Mr Nik Gowing, their prime time presenter and editor.

To verify my contributions I rang up the BBC's Delhi office and again the lady who answered was Seema Chishti. She was very polite this time and asked if I made a documentary in Ayodhya, to which I explained what I had done there. She suggested that I speak to the 'bosses'. I do not know what was wrong with me, but I had never dared to speak to the white bosses in the BBC's India office. Perhaps the hurt of my discontinuation from the internship was there in my mind. Also, somewhere I thought that my little experiences in Ayodhya were not sufficient to enable me to speak to such senior people in such a big organization. But what I continued to do was make phone calls, which were sometimes attended to, and sometimes ignored. Most of the time they were considered spam calls.

I had met some Associated Press journalists in Ayodhya, like the person who had given gave me a ride to Lucknow. There was also fresh news there for me. The head of Zee News, (who was earlier the team leader of English bulletins, and about whom I have mentioned in previous chapters, had joined the Associated Press). She was married now. This link was sufficient for me to approach the AP so one fine morning I landed in the AP office in Zorbagh, in central Delhi. I never realized that I might be imposing myself before such a big organization and such a nice lady. A very civilized lady she is and was warm and helpful to my problems. She attended me and I congratulated her on her marriage and then put forward my problem that I was in need of a job. Maybe, I think it was not the right time to ask such silly questions but to share my feelings on her marriage. So, as I was doing before asking all the individuals in the media circles, I requested if she could do anything for me. She listened very carefully and where everybody had rejected me, she consoled and assured me, but did not promise anything as she was also new in AP. It was enough for me that someone had heard me and given me a full fifteen minutes to express my feelings. There was life and motivation in her words and when I returned home I was more determined.

My next destination was to meet the magnet of media, Rajdeep Sardesai, the then political editor of NDTV, a busy man.

He was a man who was born and brought up in a truly western culture. He was born in Ahmedabad, Gujarat, to a Goan father, the former Indian Test cricketer Dilip Sardesai, and a Gujarati mother, Nandini Sardesai, a Mumbai based activist in Mumbai and former head of the Department of Sociology at St. Xavier's College, Mumbai. Rajdeep Sardesai attained his schooling up to ICSE at the Campion School in Mumbai, did two years of ISC in the Cathedral School, also in Mumbai, and then completed a bachelor's course in Economics from St. Xavier's College. And as I said, he was more inclined towards higher studies in a British atmosphere, so then he went to University College, Oxford, getting degrees in Bachelor of Arts, Master of Arts, and Bachelor of Civil Law. Following his father's footsteps he represented Oxford University Cricket Club in county cricket and played seven matches for them as a batsman in the English summer of 1987. Rajdeep Sardesai switched from print media to television journalism in 1994 when he joined as Political Editor of New Delhi Television (NDTV).

Rajdeep Sardesai is a man who understood the strength of television and also the needs of Indian news viewers. He realized the need for an international television channel with an Indian flavor, and to nourish this dream he quit NDTV to start his own company, Global Broadcast News (GBN), in collaboration with the American giant CNN and Raghav Bahl's TV18.

The latter broadcasts the Indian Edition of CNBC called CNBC-TV18, the Hindi consumer channel, CNBC Awaaz and an international channel, SAW. The news channel with Sardesai as the Editor-in-Chief has been named CNN-IBN which went on air on 17 December, 2005. Sardesai has won several national and international awards for his journalism and is the former President of the Editors Guild of India. He is also a member of the Population Council, funded by the Rockefeller Brothers Fund, which has its roots in the discredited Eugenics movement. He writes columns for leading English dailies like the Hindustan Times. The Urdu Press Club of India awarded Rajdeep with the Jasarat Award in 2003 for the coverage ofing the Gujarat riots. He has been conferred the honourable "Padmashri" award by the Government of India in 2008, for his excellence in journalism. Under Rajdeep's leadership CNN IBN has also won Asian Television Awards which recognizes excellence in production, programming and performance.

But for me, I was going to meet a humble man who had inspired me many times, received my phone calls, and gave me the time to meet. This time again he called me up into his office at 11:00 am. I had courage and confidence which had been generated by the lady at AP and also what I had learnt about TV journalism in Ayodhya with me, but above all I had a feeling of greatness, a feeling that one feels when he is meeting a great person. Enlightened, I entered NDTV's Archana Complex in Greater Kailash and realized it was difficult for me to control my heartbeat.

I was made to wait, relaxed at the reception and walked around before finally I saw the big man himself coming out. With warmness in his gestures, he smiled, shook my hand and sat down with me on a sofa. I told him that I was looking forward to a chance to assist him and work with him. He very humbly asked me to come the next day and to e-mail my resume to him.

This was something which was enough for me, enough for me to start dreaming and flying in the sky. I was on cloud nine when I entered my house. Soon I dispatched my resume to Mr Sardesai on his NDTV e-mail and waited.

The next morning I collected all my certificates and reached the NDTV office just to find that a fresh lot of students from Kamla Nehru College were also invited to be interviewed. I found that these freshly passed students were very excited, not because they were getting an opportunity to work in NDTV, but due to the fact that they had got an opportunity to meet the charismatic Mr Sardesai. Soon we all were all invited to the first floor of the office and from where I could see that some of the interns who had worked with me in Zee News, (the Symbiosis lot who were with me in the Campaign Trail team), had already started working at NDTV.

We all were all asked to wait, and I could see through the glass partition what was going on inside the cabin in which Rajdeep was sitting with another prominent member of NDTV, and anchor Sonia Verma. We were being called in one by one, and were all eagerly asking many questions from the candidate who had just come out to get to know what was asked. I had a looked over my resume and was finding it difficult to control my breath and when finally my turn came, I was feeling that my heart will would jump out of my mouth when I entered the cabin. Rajdeep Sardesai was busy tracking news on his monitor and it was Sonia Verma who asked me to sit. She went over my resume and then Rajdeep turned towards me and said, "We will get back to you."

I was literally sweating when I came out of the NDTV office and caught a bus to return home. Two days later I called Rajdeep to ask what had happened about my case and he said, "We have not shortlisted you." And that was the end to my efforts to gain a second entry into TV news. Somehow I tried to accept the truth that I was perhaps not fit for my dreams which now I dared not to nurture.

This was a debacle for me, but rigid and determined I kept writing reports and dispatching them to Rajdeep Sardesai and Nik Gowing, without realizing that they were all considered as spam mails, and most of the time were deleted by the recipients. I also extended this habit to Anita Pratap, the Associated Press lady, the 43rd president of USA, George W Bush (on his official e-mail id), and several other top notch media giants, until the end of 2010.

AJE photo

Demise of a Monk and the Media glare in Ayodhya

My next visit to Ayodhya was only next year, in July 2003, when the media started broadcasting the news of Ramchandra Das Paramhans' poor health. I had not been able to find a regular job after I was rejected by Rajdeep, but stuck to the habit of writing reports and sending these e-mail dispatches to almost two dozen top media people and organizations across the globe. Somehow it was satisfying my journalistic instincts. In this timespan of a year and a half, between March 2002 to July 2003, I stayed with my brother's family in Noida and occupied myself by hunting for a job and dispatching said e-mails to all these places and individuals.

So, when I got the news of Ramchandra Paramhans' illness, I readily boarded a train to Ayodhya, my birthplace. Most of the news men who were gathered in Ayodhya were from local newspapers and TV channels, as they were frequently shuffling between Ayodhya and PGI Lucknow, where Ramchandra Paramhans was getting treatment. A couple of times he had been admitted and then discharged after initially getting treatment. This was around the last week of July when both national and international media had started beaming in on the pilgrim town. But this time the media was not going to get any breaking news or exclusives on the Ram temple/Babri mosque issue, as the man behind the movement was ill.

I visited Ramchandra Paramhhans and met his PRO Vimlendra Mishra, who also happened to be my friend. He told me that the monk was in poor health and that his blood pressure was shooting to abnormal levels. I requested if I could speak to the monk, but he was unable to due to his illness and was confined to an AC room on the first floor of the Digamabar Akhara. Many top leaders from the BJPand VHP were visiting him, and soon national and international media persons started arriving again in Ayodhya and occupying all the hotels and lodges in the twin towns.

I was expecting the media gathering to be almost double in comparison to the previous year's 'Ram Shila Poojan' event, in case something unfortunate happened to Paramhans. TV media was already there broadcasting speculation about his health and what would happen next if Pramhans died. One such TV crew was from *NDTV*. They had stationed themselves on the banks of the Saryu on the Ghats of 'Ram Ki Paudi'. The correspondent with this team was Shikha Trivedi, a renowned journalist renowned on social issues. Just to brief you about her – Shikha Trivedi is one of those journalists in India who talks about rural problems, drought, gender equality issues and women empowerment. She is a sharp political journalist who carries out a lot of research for her reports. She was married to the late Mr Surendra Pratap Singh, the man who conceptualized *Aaj Tak*. This time she was in Ayodhya.

Knowing she was part of Rajdeep Sardesai's team, I thought of going to meet her on the banks of the Saryu from where she was doing live broadcasts each evening. I went there and immediately asked if I could assist her for a few days. I told her how I knew her political editor Rajdeep Sardesai. She agreed that I could stand there and watch whatever she was doing and reporting. That evening she planned to interview leaders of both sections who were involved in the Ram Temple/Babri mosque dispute. It was late in the evening when Vinay Katiyar, the leader from the Hindu extremist party 'Bajrang Dal', and the BJP member of parliament from Faizabad and Hasim Ansari of the Babari Masjid action committee came to the venue on the Ghats of 'Ram ki Paudi', where the OB van and NDTV team were stationed.

I observed that Shikha Trivedi had a diary with her in which she probably had written down all her the contacts in the twin towns, as well as her plans for each day. She categorically asked both leaders how they were going to react if something unfortunate happened to Paramhans, and how they planned to maintain communal harmony in both communities. Both leaders, Vinay Katiyar and Hasim Ansari were firebrand leaders of their respective communities, and both showed their association to the cause for which they had been fighting. However, they were both reluctant to discuss the issue if it came to ensuring peace and harmony and avoided the question. When the live interview was over and Shikha Trivedi had to depart for the hotel where she was staying she gave me a ride to the centre of town, from where I took a rickshaw to my village.

The next morning, and as I had promised to Shikha Trivedi, I reached the same spot around 10:00am where the crew was waiting for me. We talked about the plan for the day and she suggested I go to cover some shots of akharas, along with the camera team, while she chalked out some more interviews. It was a great learning experience for me to work with such an eminent journalist. The next day when she departed for Delhi as she had forgot some urgent assignment there, subsequent events were supposed to be covered by another NDTV correspondent and I found that I was quite emotional.

Dominique Deluze was a cynical French documentary filmmaker, who had somehow dropped into my uncle's place, which was how I got to know he was making a documentary for a French TV channel. Not knowing that he was a cynical kind of person I joined his company for the next two days. I took him to the place where he took some shots of the stones getting reshaped for the temple construction. Then we went to meet the Raja of Ayodhya, Vimlendra Mohan Pratap Mishra and his son Yatindra Mohan Mishra. Dominique Deluze is a man who would drink cold water and hot tea together. He had his two front teeth replaced by two metal teeth. He was cynically trying to find out the reason and bias of the Hindu movement. He was in Ayodhya predicting there would be hundreds of thousands of people in the streets in case something wrong happened to the chairman of the Ram Janamabhoomi Nyas, Pramhans Ramchandra Das. We together we went to interview the Raja of Ayodhya and his son on what they thought of communal harmony.

Soon I found that it was very difficult to deal with Dominque Deluze and bear his routine, and soon parted ways with him. By this time Ramchandra Paramhans was again critical and was shifted to PGI in Lucknow.

July 31, 2003: The media, political leaders (to remind you that Atal Bihari Vajpayee's NDA government was in power at that time) and people across India were keeping a close watch on each development related to the monk's deteriorating health, as well as the subsequent consequences in case of his death. And as expected, the date of July 31, 2003 had something hidden for the expectations of the Hindus who believed in the idea that the Ram Temple must be constructed in Ayodhya.

Early in the morning the monk's condition worsened beyond the control of the doctors and he took his last breath in the PGI, Lucknow around 9:00am. The news of his death soon spread in all quarter, television channels jumping on the story, along with detailed coverage on his association with the Ram Temple movement. It was something that was expected. The monk was 90 years old and had devoted 70 years of his life to the Ram Temple movement. Born as Chandreshwar Tiwari in 1913 into a prosperous Brahmin family in the eastern state of Bihar, Ramchandra Das Paramhans had studied Sanskrit, the Vedas and other Indian scriptures at Kashi. When his parents pressed him to get married, he rebelled and moved to Ayodhya, where he became a holy man, or sadhu, claiming that he had been destined from before birth to build a temple on the site of the Babri Mosque.

As the head of the Ramjanmabhoomi Nyas (the Rama Birthplace Temple Trust), a powerful Hindu group, Paramhans led the battle for a Rama temple for more than 70 years. With his flowing white beard, matted hair, a a piece of cloth tied around his waist and beads hung round his chest, he looked the archetypal Hindu holy man. Rather less typical was his reputation for tantrums and rejection of the Hindu teaching philosophy that there are many ways leading to God. His dedication to the cause was fanatical: "Even if god Rama comes and says he was not born here, I will not believe him," he once said.

In 1934, he played a prominent role in the violent attempts by Hindu activists to take over the mosque, which left the structure damaged and also ended in the imposition of a collective fine on the people of Ayodhya. After independence, in 1949, he was instrumental in 1949 in installing a statue of Rama under the mosque dome, and the following year launched a court case staking a claim to the land in the name of the deity. He fought the case for years before withdrawing it in the early 1980s.

Soon obituaries and condolences started beaming in on TV channels. Prime Minister Atal Bihari Vajpayee was among the several leaders who paid glowing tributes to Mahant Ramchandra Paramhans.

"His death has shocked me profoundly. He was extremely benevolent towards me. When I was going on a foreign visit, he had specially sent his blessings," he said in his message. "Paramhans was firm like a mountain and affectionate like River Sarayu. His contribution towards the Ramjanambhoomi movement will be etched in golden letters. I offer my humble tributes at his feet," the Prime Minister said.

Then Deputy Prime Minister Lal Krishna Advani said, "The death of Mahant Ramchandra Paramhans has deeply shocked me. Paramhans was very firm on whatever he said, and was kind and affectionate to all. Even at the age of ninety years, he was active till he breathed his last."

"His contribution to the Shri Ramjanambhoomi movement cannot be assessed easily and it will be written in history in golden letters. While paying my humble tribute to Paramhans, I feel we have lost a great saint who sacrificed his life for the movement," Advani said.

Bharatiya Janata Party General Secretary Mukhtar Abbas Naqvi said, "He was not only a religious leader, but also very patriotic. A moderate, he was a crucial link towards finding an amicable solution to the vexed (Ayodhya) issue."

Describing Paramhans as the 'leading pillar' of the Ram Janambhoomi movement, Vishwa Hindu Parishad joint general secretary Onkar Bhave said it would work with full strength towards the realisation of his dream of a grand Ram temple at Ayodhya.

By evening Ayodhya was converted into a fortress, and almost two dozen TV channels from national and international media agencies had occupied every hotel, lodge and dharamshala across the twin towns. Name a TV channel and it was there. Ayodhya had turned into a media and political hub within twelve hours. The reason for this was that the Atal Bihari led BJP–NDA government was in power, which supported the Ram Temple movement. All were predicting a big political gathering during the last ritual ceremony for the monk. We all waited for his body to arrive at Digambar Akhara, which all of sudden had become a central place where the media and political leaders had started to arrive. All his followers and people from across the twin towns had already gathered there, and more were arriving from different parts of the country. By the next morning Ayodhya was a place where people in general, political leaders from the state and central government and religious leaders from different temples, math and akharas had arrived.

But, above all, there was a media glare in Ayodhya, the first of its kind after the 1992 Babri demolition.

The Sadhu Samaj (Society of Sadhus) have a tradition of carrying the dead body of their guru in a state of meditation (Samadhi Awastha), rather than in a lying down state, to the place where the last rites are performed. The next day when the procession for the last rites started from Digambar Akhara, Paramhans Ramchandra Das's body was kept in 'Samdhi Awastha'. He looked like a monk sitting on his chariot, and proceeding to visit his disciples and maths.

I joined the procession along with the monk's PRO, Vimlendra Mishra, and as was my habit, I dispatched e-mails and made calls to different media organizations and individuals, keeping them informed on whatever was going on in Ayodhya. I did not know they were already there in the gathering of more than two dozen media organizations. We were all informed that the leaders from the center would be paying their tributes and were coming to Ayodhya within the next couple of hours. This meant that the media had to focus more on the speeches of these leaders and less on the monk's ritual ceremony.

The security was at its best, keeping in mind that any spark, any fiery speech could have triggered violence. The security forces had been deployed at each corner of the twin towns of Ayodhya and Faizabad, and across whole state of Uttar Pradesh.

The procession, along with the dead body of the monk, reached the banks of the Saryu at a designated spot where his pyre was to be lit. And during this two and half hour journey from the Digamabar Akhara to the banks of the Saryu, I dispatched all that I saw to dozens of individuals and organizations in media circles.

When the procession reached the banks of the Saryu, I saw the impact of the charismatic monk on the public and the leaders. Some 50,000 people had gathered from all across the state. Media persons were given a proper building and along with its rooftop to cover the last rites, with a stage made from where the Prime Minister of India, Deputy Prime Minister and other political leaders from the state and center, religious leaders and monks could stand and speak.

Somehow I managed to get into a place from where I could see the monk's body laid down on a pyre and all were waiting for the PM and Deputy PM to arrive. They and other political leaders were coming by road from Lucknow. What I could easily observe was more than two dozen TV cameras stationed on the rooftop of the designated building and almost the same number who were in search of a place on the ground.

Soon a big convoy with almost 30-40 vehicles arrived at the place of the last rites and all top political leaders of the NDA government (including the PM and Deputy PM), VHP leaders, RSS leaders and leaders from extremist Hindu outfits groups emerged and gathered on the stage erected for them.

As they gave their condolences and tributes to the monk and showed their commitment to build a magnificent Ram Temple, I was amazed to see that a democratic government was wholeheartedly standing behind and supporting them.

The pyre was lit and the fumes emerging from the monk's soul were synchronizing with the supreme power and, as the sun dropped, I saw Hindu masses were also dropping one of the prominent hopes in the Ram Temple movement.

The sun had set in the western sky and all the top leaders of center and state, along with the media, had left the venue. There were just the remains of the monk who had seen the fame and glory in his lifetime, built on the foundation of emotional extremism, which had changed the political destiny of a country, and which had forced a Prime Minister and other top leaders of cabinet to come to his burning pyre and pay homage, keeping their democratic dilemmas aside.

The Second Phase of Joblessness and Relocating to Bangalore

Two weeks later, when Ayodhya returned to normalcy, I too packed up my bags and returned to my hub in Noida – my elder brother's residence. I appreciate that all of my family members including my parents and my brother were not questioning my cynicism to go to places and dispatch reports without being linked with any organization, without a valid ID card and without being an employee of any media house. It all was due to my craze and my cynicism that I wanted to work as a journalist, and I stayed firm to my inner calling.

Soon, after returning from Ayodhya, I found that the big black question was still there – to find a regular job. The media contacts that I had developed in Ayodhya were not working anymore, and each knock on the doors of media companies had remained unattended. I struggled, fought and kept asking for a job from whomsoever I met for the next year.

I tried to overshadow my worries with pleasant and beautiful face of little dark and tall girl which has occupied my conscience for past several months and decided to be frequent to South Campus.

Valentine day was coming close and Ii once gain decided to express my deep love for her.But it was very difficult task to see her in South Campus.When ever I went to South Ccampus she was either busy in her studies or tucked inside Geetanjali Hostel. One day I again decided to stay late and leave a message for her to meet her.

There was a busy market place near South Campus known as Staya Niketan. I went there and stayed till 09:00 PM and all of sudden I saw here emerging from other side with another boy.She again passed a lope sided smile at me.The boy asked me to join them and we sat on a table to sip a cup of tea.I was very desperate to express my love for her almost like if I will not do that my I will miss my train. I wanted to lock this chapter of my life and moment for ever.So I started spaeaking whatever came in my mind and spoke close to five minutes.She listened me and gave a beautiful smile and soon we three departed.

I returned home thinking how to carry this chapter forward but the big question which I had to face was about a foothold, a job and this was the second phase of my joblessness.

My elder brother, his wife and my parents were the ones who were consoling me all through these days. But there is something called luck which had a personal enmity with me. I kept calling the media houses and individuals each day and knocking on the doors of each opportunity, but somehow my voice was not being heard.

And during such depressing days the only hopes were my brother and my parents. One day I got the news that my brother had got promoted and was set to join another software giant, Intel, in Bangalore. He was insisting that our parents should also accompany him while he left it to my will whether I would also go along or keep struggling in the big bad media world, as I felt all my hopes had died.

We were joined by a new entrant in my family. My elder brother's wife had delivered a cute prince to whom we all had named 'Sagun,' as he was the first baby boy to for the next generation of my family.

My elder brother has been my inspiration since childhood. We are more like friends and less like brothers. A very hardworking person, he was the one whom my father trusted a lot. I have seen him grow mature at a very early stage of his life, and he was the hope and inspiration for my entire village.

He had been taking care of his own academic expenditure from when he was still in graduation college. He finised his schooling from the Government Intermediate College in Faizabad, and I remember when I joined the same school in class 9th standard, he had taken me on his bicycle to and from school which was about six to seven kilometers from our village. However whenever the situation became worse in my village and we were sheltered by one of our relatives in Faizabad, he would often shout at me for getting late for school, but never forgot to take me on his bicycle.

Later, he completed his graduation from a college in Faizabad and an M.Sc in Electronics from a University which I have mentioned in a later chapter in this story. His love for academic books and the desire to work hard had got him into one of the best Universities in India – Banaras Hindu University. Here he did his Ph D on micro sensors. I remember we all were very emotional when he departed for IT-BHU Banaras to pursue his dream from IT-BHU. Soon I followed at regular intervals to see him and soon got a place in the Journalism program of BHU, but which I later changed to Lucknow University. BHU possesses a strong backbone of academic excellence and was founded by the renowned freedom fighter Pt. Mahaman Madan Mohan Malviya. It is one of the premier institutions imparting higher education in humanities, social sciences, sciences, engineering and medical sciences. My elder brother had a nose for scientific research. He had presented many research papers and filed several patents during his Ph.D studies. Whenever I visited him I found him absorbed in his studies, preparing for his examinations and busy with the laboratory researches for his doctorate. He finished his Ph.D in record time and was offered a lectureship in the Birla Institute of Technology and Sciences(BITS)-Pilani. He later joined an MNCs keeping in mind the responsibilities he had held towards his family.

His wife and my Bhabhi, had also been good in academics. She finished her M.Sc. from the same university in Faizabad, where we had all studied, before marrying my brother. She finally joined him in the same software firm. A very lovable lady and caring as well, she never questioned my joblessness when I was rejected by almost all the individuals and media organizations. They together make a lovable, adorable and responsible family and to date are the financial backbone for all of us. They have also given us two adorable children – Sagun and Ishani (Ishani was born in Bangalore).

One night we were all sitting together at our rented Noida house discussing our relocation to Bangalore, when Sagun, who was by now one and half years old, asked me in his innocent way to come to Bangalore with them. I had no hope left in Delhi that I would get a foothold in the media industry. Maybe something would bring about a change for me in Bangalore, perhaps my luck would give me a chance that I finally decided to accompany my parents and brother's family to Bangalore. This is how I planned to leave the city for which I had a dream – a beautiful dream.

My brother, his wife, Sagun and my mother left for Bangalore a month ahead of us and stayed in the Leela Place before finding a beautiful ground floor house for all of us in Indira Nagar near the BTM layout. My father and I stayed in Noida for our belongings and new Maruti Zen car had reached Bangalore. And then finally the day came when I had to say goodbye to the city where I had nurtured a failed dream to get into the media industry. What I had with me were a few phone numbers, some contacts, some addresses and some sweet and sour memories of individuals who had helped me and of some of those who had shattered my dream to make it a success in the big bad media world. This was around May 2004 when my destiny was carrying me to another dream city, the southern plateau part of India, carrying a man with broken wings who had finally found hope for his life. When I was packing my luggage I could feel sadness for this city, for its people and also for the failure which was destined for a longer time period. I cried that night as I had to leave the city and thought that I will not be able to see that little dark but tall girl whom I have bestowed my love again..

My father and I boarded the train bound for Bangalore from New Delhi railway station. I could feel the pain of failure in my eyes. My father, who was now growing old, but still had the imprints on his face of the battles he fought for in life, for all so that he could provide us to nurture all my siblings and make us into good human beings. An iron man, I would say he gave me company, mentored me and shared all of my sufferings by keeping himself in front to avoid any problems for any of us. This remarkable man was my partner in the almost two day long journey through the changing landscape and from the north to the west and finally to the south of India. The train had caught its speed. I looked towards my father. He was busy arranging his sheets and asked me to do the same as well.

My father was a second son to his parents in a family of four brothers and one sister. He is an articulate person, a very religious man who is passionate about his work. He is honest, simple and has always been pushing all of us for higher studies and teaching us to be good human beings. He hardly ever missed a visit to the Hanuman Garhi in Ayodhya every Tuesday. He was born and brought up in the village where we all were later born. His father, and my grandfather, were Gram Pradhan. My father had grown up under strict religious guidelines and in a typical Brahmin cultural environment, which he still followed. He had witnessed many unwanted and unpleasant moments in his life while in his struggle to educate all his sons and daughters and make them good human beings.

He has seen his children's deaths, he has battled with limited resources, but has successfully overcome all the obstacles which came his way during the tough turns of his life. His primary focus was to give the best education to his children, and to give him them a better life and finally to see all of them develop into good human beings, which I believe he has successfully managed with all of us. When situations became adverse in my village (due to caste violence), he sent me and my brother to one of our relative's house to make us feel secure. I remember that he never shouted at any of us, nor had he ever raised his hands to any of us. We lived in a joint family with two of his younger brothers and their families to whom he often supported with all his capacity. In our village his advice in still holds value, and his simplicity is always adored. He did all he could within his financial limits as a school teacher and then as Sub Divisional Inspector of Schools (SDI) to make all of us feel good, educated and proud.

He was married to my mother who had supported him step by step, in odd and even times, through tough and critical phases of life. I never saw her fighting with or complaining to my father when we were facing difficulties. My mother belongs to another reputed Brahmin family from the same area and she had seen some unpleasant turns in her life with her parental family. Her only brother, and my Mamaji, had served in a directorial position in the IGFRI (Indian Grassland and Fodder Research Institute) in Jhansi. Both my parents had thrown away their desires many times in order to give us the best of in life, and thank god they both succeeded. My father often claimed that he could not give anything to my mother just because he had to raise his children, and in return my mother would say that all my father's 'Poojas' (prayers) were meant for their children.

My father, accompanying me in the train, looked towards me and asked me to arrange the sheets provided by the railway staff. I followed his advice. He then asked if I wanted something to eat. We ordered dinner and waited for it to arrive. While my father went to freshen himself, I kept thinking about what had gone wrong with me that I had not been able to penetrate the media industry, why people had refused me, and why I could not convince the people with whom I had met.

We ate our dinner and soon my father was asleep. I took out a book from my bag and tried to focus on reading, but found that I was unable to concentrate. The denials, the refusals and the departure from my dream city – of Delhi were haunting me. A few faces which kept occupying my brain were those of Rajdeep Sardesai, the AP lady and Ami. Soon I too fell asleep.

My father woke me up at 7:00am and asked to have my tea. He had already woken up and, as was his habit, had freshened up. Very gently he looked at me and reminded me that we had reached Nagpur. All of sudden I woke up, looked out the window and found that the train had stopped at Nagpur. Coolies, vendors, railway book stalls and shops selling fresh oranges were what I saw on the platform. I was thinking about how Nagpur had stayed sheltered and was now a hub of the Rashtriya Swayamsevak Sangh (RSS), a Hinduist organization which was said to be behind the demolitions of the Babri Mosque in Ayodhya.

I sipped the tea offered by my father, while he kept telling me how my elder brother had performed well and how he took care of all of us. I agreed and told him that I would try to do something new in Bangalore, not knowing what was the best thing I could do in an unknown city. We talked on different issues ranging from politics to family, and from life in Delhi to our new destination – Bangalore.

The train had started moving and as I observed that the soil had changed color from a darkish brown to blackish, in this part of Mahrashtara, I thought that something would also change the colors in my life.

We took our lunch served by the Indian Railways and rested for a couple of hours. I woke up to have evening tea when I noticed that the train had reached Anant in Andhra Pradesh. The change in attire and language was evident and was telling us that we had reached a different shade of India. Bada Sambhar, Idley Sambhar and Aaloo Bonda were the key items being sold at on the railway platform. My father and I had a couple of plates of these items, and I then tried to concentrate on my book which was talking about how versatile Indian culture and its people were.

Around 7:30 am we reached Seccuenderabad, the twin town of Hyderabad, the capital of Andhra Pradesh. My father told me that within the next 10 to 12 hours we would reach Bangalore. This part of India was new for me and I found that the specialty with train travel is that you get plenty of opportunities to meet new people and see all the places which fell en-route. My father ordered dinner for this night as well and as we waited, kept ourselves busy talking about the new people and places we were visiting on this journey. Listening to my father, I found words of encouragement, advice and appreciation for my elder brother. He kept reminding me that I must follow my brother's footsteps.

We had our dinner together and as we were to reach Bangalore the next morning we went to sleep in eagerness to meet everybody in the family. I found that the worries and pains of Delhi were slipping from my mind, while the eagerness to see this new place and meet everyone else in the family was somehow trying to console me. The next morning he woke me up, asked me to get freshened up and have my tea as we were about to reach our destination.

The train reached Bangalore City station at 9:30am. As the train was slowing down I saw my brother waving at us and as the train stopped he rushed towards our bogie we were boarding. He had come alone to receive us as his wife had gone to the office. Soon we came out of the station where a hired taxi was waiting for us. I had reached Bangalore, the city where I hoped for a new life and new wings for my desires. Everything was appearing to be in good shape and form, the weather, the people. But my worries were still with me hoping to vanish to give an avenue to hope and success.

My elder brother had got a beautiful ground floor house in Indira Nagar near the BTM layout. We had plenty of space for all of us and for Sagun to play around, but my brother had a very busy schedule. Both my brother and his wife were still working with Intel corp, and I had the whole day for planning new avenues in a new city. On the first floor of this double story house was an aging couple and the owners of the house were staying were Tamils. The landlady was a doctor and quite often came down to meet all of us. I chalked out my daily routine and that included searching the newspapers, as well as roaming around the city looking for a job. Unlike Delhi, Bangalore had little to offer in terms of the media industry and its expansion. There were state bureaus which were located in Bangalore but they had limited space, requirements and staff. Bangalore as a city is a beautifully crafted one. Vast gardens, wide roads, disciplined traffic, great pieces of architecture and design of buildings, and moreover it was a hub of India's IT revolution' one finds a different mood in this city. Gentle people from all corners of India, workaholics but patient.

I liked roaming around the city and enjoyed a lot in the different atmosphere. Early in the morning each day I would come out of the house, run a kilometer in the healthy weather, and then after having breakfast would go out looking how to explore. Initially, I visited media houses like the Times of India, NDTV and a couple of other news organizations. I mentioned before these people, what little I had done in Delhi, but as I said they required a limited staff and so it was quite difficult to get a foothold.

In mean time I also tried to make a touch base with that little dark but tall girl but could not get success.She was still there deep in my conscience. I started writing to her on her e-mail but that also failed and no reply came from her.

This was becoming impossible for me everyday. I started smoking quite frequently, but without bringing it to the notice of my family. I felt I was going through a phase of restlessness. Cyber cafes in the Thipsandra market became my next destination to search for whatever seemed news to me. All of sudden I started realizing that I had lots of information on current affairs and had a lot of contacts in the form of e-mails and phone numbers. But what to do with this information and these global contacts when they were accepting all my e-mails as spam.

One fine day when I was in the cyber cafe I thought of the unorganized information and contacts and that I must utilize the art of e-mailing, which I had learnt from Anita Pratap, into a channelized form. And after a week of brainstorming I finalized an e-mail based program which was sent to almost two dozen individuals including Rajdeep Sardesai, the AP lady, Nik Gowing, and the 43rd President of USA ,- George W Bush at his official e-mail and organizations across the globe. I named it "The Nose of the News", and I carried it on till the end of 2010.

The Nose of the News

My idea was to search out websites, books, newspapers and television programs, and analyse their content and then dispatch it to these individuals and organizations who often considered my e-mails as worthless and a waste of time. At the end of every episode, I wrote:

Dear All,

"The Nose of the News" is a result of three years research work by me and is an exercise to select the 100 most influential individuals and reports of this world. The effort is an unbiased exercise to bring out the ablest brains without political, regional, communal, religious and racial bias.

The idea I have already brainstormed seeks assurances from all of you to carry on this work to mark the present era legends. This is the writer's promise that it is so far an unfunded work but bears scientific facts about the evolution of the human brain.

I request the liberty from all my readers to allow me this long series which deals with both the sides of human behaviour and breed… the positive and negative, as they make the world together.

The long series would be sent to selected individuals across the globe, also there would be a trial to send it to those individuals/organisations who would make their valuable presence as selected members of this list of 100.

I would be happy to receive any queries from individuals receiving it as my readers.

Lastly, my practice is to let the world know what actually takes to be above normal in the world.

With warm regards

RATNESH DWIVEDI

15th AUGUST 2004

Then there were the e-mail dispatches. For your convenience I am giving here the extract of sixteen dispatches that I filed between 2004 and 2010.

Dispatch-1

The Economics of Political South Asia

There is hardly anything to recall from the 1980's South Asian economics boom. India, which makes up a larger part of the region, its neighboring countries having fatal religious tendencies, and politics is mostly governed by these sentiments and, thus, are the economics. The Hindus who are basically defenders of their faith and the Muslims who haves chosen an attacking mode to defend their religious identit, two chief religions in this region. Economic supremacy was always considered an area of selected individuals, and also which is also limited to the upper crest of society.

I have the Hindu faith and also the memories of bloodshed. Until my school days I had very little knowledge of economics as a subject. My interest started growing in this subject only when I was convinced by my siblings that economics are more of a social concern and less of limited breed of intellectuals.

The economics of political South Asia or Finance, Business, Marketing and Sales as it is called more generally, has now been modified by many new terminologies and has taken a front row within the last few years. Even sciences, which allows humans to grow towards perfection, has taken a back seat. Everything is now governed by Economics.

And new media, step by step, plays a phenomenal role in defining the society as these terminologies wish. In pre-liberalization South Asia there were not many brands of goods and appliances which one may recall that Tatas, Birlas, Singhanias, Ambanis were the business tycoons. Ambassadors, Fiats and Marutis were the cars on the roads. Teaching, Medical and Engineering were the jobs one would prefer to opt for, and the Times of India, Hindustan Times and Doordarshan were your sources of information. These were things to remember and use.

But the swift changes and feeling towards the western world has expanded the mind and mode of living among the diverse population in South Asia. I was guided by one of my UK based friends to know about the possibilities of newspaper access on my computer. Washington Post, NY Times, USA Today, The Guardian, The Independent and many more newspapers are possible to go through because of the new age of economics and I may see as many brands of cars in Delhi and Bangalore as many the numerical lines I have in both of my hands in Delhi and Bangalore. My elder brother and many of his friends are enjoying highly paid MNC jobs due to the new age economics and media. I myself got an internship due to the expansion plans of the BBC World in South Asia. Hence, if we see that the listed number of companies of foreign origin are growing day by day, it gives me a feeling of hope for more good jobs in South Asia and hope for new age economics.

Now probably the phrase of Marshall that, Economics is the study of Mankind in the ordinary business of life is more diligently suited. The all time political journalists too have begun realizing the importance of Economic and Business Journalism.

A treasure book of the 1930's defines the basic code of Economics as under:

1. The need for Economics (Wants of Public) – Efforts of Selected People – Satisfaction of Whole People
2. Wants of individuals – Effort as member of group – Income Group – Income of individuals – Satisfaction of wants of individual.
3. Effort brings earnings – Income brings spending – Satisfaction

That is how Economics was defined in the 1930's:

Complex Effort;

Sheep Farmers, Wool Merchants, Spinners, Weavers, Tailors

Carrier and Bankers, Carrier and Bankers, Carrier and Bankers

That is how a standard sheep industry was defined and thus was the oil and petrol business of 1930's USA. The Mario Puzo's masterpiece novel, "'The Godfather'" defines the oil business in a similar fashion.

The beginning of Economics and its various stages are brilliantly defined in Longfellow's 'Hiwatha'.

For building his Canoe, Hiwatha took the bark from the Birch tree and fastened it over a framework of Cedar wood- like two bended bows together. The whole was bound together with roots of Larch and seams were closed with resin from the Fir tree. Lastly the finished Canoe was decorated with Hedgehos's quills, stained red, blue and yellow.

Thus the Birch Canoe was built

In the valley by River

In the bosom of Forest

And the forest life was in it

All its mystery and magic

All the lightness of Birch tree

All the toughness of Cedar

All the Larch's supple sinews

And it floated on the river

Like a yellow leaf in autumn

Like a yellow water Lilly

Longfellow's 'Hiawatha'

Hence, after years of experience of watching television channels and surfing newspapers and websites and studying the change of age-old Economics and its modification by the insertion of new age terminologies by the media, I tuned in to television which was broadcasting war time economics due to the US led attacks in Iraq. The ongoing war and transition phase in Iraq had impacted South Asia and India as well. The terrorism and the war that marred the path of Economics have taken a lethal turn and impacted the coverage of Economics in the media, which controls it.

In the middle of this, when I got to know about the expansion plans of one of the pioneers in business news providers -Reuters, in Bangalore, it left a fresh breeze in my mind and encouraged me to submit my resume at its posh office on airport road. Many jobs were posted on the internet and I was tipped by one of my friends who ran the cyber cafe in Thipsandra about the expansion of Reuters in Bangalore.

When I got a call for an interview I straight away went to the office of Reuters. A young lady called Catherine, who was from Reuters headquarters and the head database intelligence team in Bangalore, swiftly and softly called me inside. The large reception area and two floored Reuters office was beautifully designed.

She interviewed me on my interests and my basic knowledge about Economics and finance and I felt that I did not make her disappointed.

She told me that Reuters is basically a Finance and Economics news provider. It earned 90% of its revenue from the financial news market, while 10% came from other news stories that it supplied to its consumers. So far it had hired 350 employees in Bangalore, and was set to grow to 700 by the end of 2004. Mumbai, being its hub center in South Asia, now leads over the Associated Press in the South Asia region. Its worldwide tie-up with the BBC World strengthens its capacity on radio, television and broadband.

When my interview was over I found myself feeling afresh and satisfied. The behavior and soft skills of the interviewer was far better than any I had faced in many other interviews. Catherine hails from London and stays in New York. She came down to the reception to tell me how they had decorated the reception. When I was returning to my house my mind was busy thinking that while I was busy in giving an interview to Catherine, President Bush would have addressed the UN General Assembly, would have visited the New England territory from where his political rival Kerry hails, and would have signed a new order on the US's Space Exploration policies. NASA scientists would have begun various missions at NASA centers. ISS expedition – 9 astronauts would have reloaded pictures Hurricane Ivan and MNC's in Bangalore and the rest of India would have recruited many new aspirants.

The world was surely marking the beginning of a new age of Economics in political South Asia.

(This thread was dispatched by me to ten individuals including president@whiethouse.gov and many organizations as part of "The Nose of The News" on Thursday, 30 September, 2004 2:13 PM)

Dispatch-2

Democratic Dilemma (My note)

Probably Donald Rumsfeld is not in the dilemmatic state on the Al-Qaeda and Saddam Hussein link and the existence of WMD's in Iraq, but this disastrous dilemma now has occupied the minds of democrats and their policy designers. Charles is probably repeating the report of Hans Blix (UN inspector, who submitted the report on the existence of WMD's to the UN). In a sudden political move to bring down the confidence level down of US forces, Charles Dilfer is probably trying to confuse America and the rest of world. He is talking on the lines of John Kerry, who at once questions the legality of the war in Iraq, and then opines to restrict the use of German and French forces in Iraq.

(A report published in newspaper in the week of 1-7 October 2004)

EAST LANSING, Mich. – The former U.S. administrator in Iraq on Tuesday defended American actions there – a day after faulting troop strength following the ouster of Saddam Hussein.

Paul Bremer, appointed by President Bush as the head of the Iraq occupation, said on Monday that U.S. forces failed to stop widespread looting after toppling Hussein, and "paid a big price for not stopping it because it established an atmosphere of lawlessness."

During a speech on Tuesday at Michigan State University, he said his remarks had been somewhat distorted by the media.

"We certainly had enough (troops) going into Iraq, because we won the war in a very short three weeks," Bremer said.

But he added: "As I look back now ... I believe it would have been better to stop the looting.... that was found right after the war."

"One way to have stopped the looting would have been to have more troops on the ground. That's a retrospective wisdom of mine, looking backwards. I think there are enough troops there now for the job we are doing."

Bremer's latest comments differed somewhat from those of Bush campaign spokesman Brian Jones, who in an unusual public acknowledgment of internal dissent said Bremer and the military brass had clashed on troop levels.

"Ambassador Bremer differed with the commanders in the field," Jones said. "That is his right, but the president has always said that he will listen to his commanders on the ground and give them the support they need for victory."

More than a dozen people were escorted outside during Bremer's speech. One woman accused Bremer of being a war criminal and another asked, "What do you get when you go into a country and kill innocent people?"

Several people also chanted "Paul Bremer, you can't hide. We charge you with genocide."

"I'll tell you one thing, if people had behaved like this in Saddam Hussein's Iraq, they would be dead," Bremer said at one point.

(SUBS overline and lead to correct that Bremer was appointed top administrator in Iraq, sted ambassador.)

(A Report on US warfare published on the Military.com website in the week of 1-7 October 2004)

The U.S. military is fighting the most complex guerrilla war in its history, with 140,000 American soldiers trained for conventional warfare flailing against a thicket of insurgent groups with competing aims and no supreme leader.

The three dozen or so guerrilla bands agree on little beyond forcing the Americans out of Iraq.

In other U.S. wars, the enemy was clear. In Vietnam, a visible leader – Ho Chi Minh – led a single army fighting to unify the country under socialism. But in Iraq, the disorganized insurgency has no single commander, no political wing and no dominant group.

U.S. troops can't settle on a single approach to fight groups whose goals and operations vary. And it's hard to sort combatants from civilians in a chaotic land where large parts of some communities support the insurgents and others are too afraid to risk their lives to help foreigners.

"It's more complex and challenging than any other insurgency the United States has fought," said Bruce Hoffman, a RAND counterinsurgency expert who served as an adviser to the U.S.-led occupation administration.

Insurgents aren't striving for revolution as much as they are trying to spoil the U.S.-backed interim Iraqi regime by inflicting as much pain as possible on the United States and its Iraqi and foreign allies.

"We want every U.S. dog to leave the country," said an insurgent leader in Fallujah who identified himself as Abu Thar, a 45-year-old former colonel in the Iraqi army.

Beyond that, the estimated 20,000 insurgents have little in common, although groups have occasionally work together in temporary alliances of convenience. U.S. commanders describe the war as a "compound insurgency" sorted into four groups with different tactics and goals.

Three are made up of Sunni Muslims, almost all of whom are Iraqis. A fourth group is the radical cleric Muqtada al-Sadr's militia, formed of Shiite Muslims, Iraq's largest social grouping.

The largest insurgent bloc is composed of Iraqi nationalists fighting to reclaim secular power lost when Saddam Hussein was deposed in April 2003.

The second is a growing faction of hardcore fighters aligned with terrorist groups, mainly that led by Jordanian Abu Musab al-Zarqawi. The U.S. military believes they want to turn Iraq into an anti-Western stronghold that would export Islamic revolution to other countries in the region.

A third group consists of conservative Iraqis who want to install an Islamic theocracy, but who stay away from terror tactics like car bombings and the beheading of hostages.

The fourth, al-Sadr's Mahdi Army, seeks to make the cleric the nationwide Shiite leader.

Ordinary criminals also pitch in on attacks when they are paid. And gangsters who abduct people regularly sell their hostages to terror groups, which have beheaded some.

Hoffman and other independent experts feel the insurgents are succeeding, with death tolls spiraling and a guerrilla-induced climate of fear that has reduced the U.S.-led rebuilding effort to a shambles.

Abu Thar, the former colonel who was interviewed by an Iraqi reporter for The Associated Press inside insurgent-held Fallujah, gloated over his compatriots' successes, saying U.S. leaders were publicly contradicting each other about the state of the war. He also said U.S. counterattacks that kill women and children are turning public opinion in the militants' favor.

"We see the conflicting statements by the U.S. administration on Iraq as another sign of their defeat," Abu Thar said. "More volunteers are coming to us because they are fed up with the humiliation and the misdeeds of the Americans. They feel it is a national and religious duty."

Public opinion is the war's central front and it is tilting against the Americans, said James Dobbins, a former Bush administration envoy to Afghanistan and now a military analyst for RAND Corp.

"If we can't protect the population, we can't secure its trust and support," Dobbins said. "If we or the Iraqi government lose that, we ultimately lose the war."

U.S. military officers concede that the situation is tough, but they say that the intensity of the conflict could be much worse. And they argue that insurgents also alienate Iraqis with indiscriminate attacks – such as the car bombings on Thursday in Baghdad that killed 35 children and nine adults.

Commanders say U.S. strategy focuses on boosting Iraqi government control while fighting only the most necessary battles.

"History is replete with insurgencies that failed," one general said privately during a discussion of Iraq.

History is also replete with insurgencies that triumphed. Vietnamese guerrillas ousted the United States in 1973. Afghan militias similarly embarrassed the Soviet Union in 1989.

If Iraqi insurgents succeed in toppling the U.S.-backed government, analysts believe the stark differences in the groups' goals could lead to a civil war that might break Iraq into rival fiefs.

Bad decisions by the U.S.-led occupation administration are widely blamed for stoking the war. Those cited most often are the disbanding of the Iraqi army and the banning of Saddam's political leaders from public life, both of which are said to have converted potential allies into enemies.

Independent analysts say 16 months of escalating warfare by U.S. troops with little practical experience in fighting insurgents have made clear the difficulty of defeating militants who mount attacks while hiding and moving among civilians.

The analysts say that the most promising chance for victory lies in U.S.-trained Iraqi security forces. U.S. and Iraqi troops reclaimed the city of Samarra from insurgents over the weekend, but it's unclear how much fighting was done by the Iraqis.

"The United States can buy the Iraqi government time to get organized, but the U.S. has become too unpopular and lost too much support among the population to be able to itself win a counterinsurgency campaign," Dobbins said.

The U.S. military has few homegrown models for counterinsurgency success. Its last two major campaigns – in Somalia in 1993 and in Vietnam in the 1960s and 1970s – failed.

Both times, a tenacious enemy fought hard enough to force U.S. troops from its soil. No one has said that the Iraqi insurgents are as tough as the Communist Viet Cong, and the United States had little incentive to stay in Somalia once the militias made things difficult.

"Vietnam was not easy, but it was certainly far less complex and more straightforward," Hoffman said.

If the insurgents are unorganized and unfocused, their tactics are classic. Guerrilla wars often feature car bombings, assassinations and abductions in the early stages, said Richard K. Betts, director of the Institute for War and Peace Studies at Columbia University.

As the militants gain strength, they progress to fielding combat troops, Betts said. In Iraq, large formations of Iraqi insurgents have met with mixed success. U.S. commanders claim their troops killed more than 4,000 al-Sadr fighters in April and August. But Sunni fighters in Fallujah and other cities have mounted daring attacks and melted away with few killed.

(A Report on training of Muslim youth by Al-Qaeda published on Military.com website in the week of 1-7 October 2004)

After leaving university, Atta-ur Rehman traded his jeans and T-shirts for a beard and cap, his civil-service aspirations for a martyr's spot in heaven.

He used to spend his time playing cricket, but he is now in a Pakistani jail facing a death sentence on terrorism charges. Mr. Rehman, along with nine other "comrades," is charged with carrying out a deadly June attack against a senior Pakistani Army general in Karachi. The general escaped narrowly but 10 people, including seven soldiers, were killed.

Rehman's circle calls themselves the 'Jundullah' (God's Army) and have close ties to Al Qaeda. Most are young, educated men, whom Rehman allegedly sent to training camps in Pakistan's remote tribal areas.

Rehman doesn't fit the mold of the typical Al Qaeda leader. Traditionally, most were Arabs who gained status by resisting the Russians in Afghanistan in the 1980s. Younger, educated recruits tapped for suicide missions like 9/11 typically came from Middle Eastern countries with long histories of pan-Islamic resistance. What sets this new breed apart is that they are joining from places like Pakistan, where the focus has been on regional grievances, like independence for the disputed area of Kashmir. But as the Al Qaeda leadership ranks begin to thin, men like Rehman are starting to climb the ladder.

"It is a new generation of Al Qaeda," says Riffat Hussain, a leading defense and security analyst based in Islamabad, Pakistan. "These are new converts to Al Qaeda. They may have no links with Al Qaeda in the past, but now they are willing to sacrifice their lives for the cause, as they feel that Al Qaeda is the name of defiance to the West. They are young and angry, and their number has swelled in the aftermath of the US invasion of Iraq."

A voice on an audiotape last weekend, purported to be that of Ayman al-Zawahiri, Osama bin Laden's deputy, called on young Muslims to continue the global fight even if Al Qaeda's leaders are killed or captured. It is people like Rehman and his colleagues that Mr. Zawahiri could have been talking about.

Police here suggest that Pakistan's newly organized jihadis and educated radicals might number in the hundreds. Police say that more than 600 suspected Al Qaeda militants have been rounded up by security forces over the past three years.

Two types of recruits

Mohammad Naeem Noor Khan, the 28-year-old known as Al Qaeda's 'computer man', is among them. A middle-class engineering graduate, Mr. Khan is believed to have played an important role in planning terrorist attacks in the US and Britain, before he was arrested in Lahore on July 13(?).

Khan visited Afghanistan during his student days and later became a bridge between Al Qaeda leaders and their operatives. He helped Al Qaeda operatives send encrypted messages over the Internet.

"His journey to Al Qaeda started from outside a mosque in his Karachi neighborhood where he met extremists," says his old friend named Khurram. He watched his friend's transformation but "never imagined that he would become such a man."

Under interrogation, Khan exposed part of Al Qaeda's intricate web of contacts in Pakistan, Britain, and the US. The information led to the July arrest of Tanzanian terror suspect Ahmed Khalfan Ghailani and a top Al Qaeda operative, Musa el Hindi, in Britain.

"There are two types of recruits," says a senior Pakistani counterterrorism investigator. "There are Islamist-educated young men from middle-class and upper -middle-class families whose feelings are ignited in Islamic congregations at private houses, mosques, and madrassahs, and are subsequently picked up by Al Qaeda men from there," he says. "Then there are jihadis who were trained by Arabs and the Taliban in Afghanistan and have now been approached by Al Qaeda operatives or their trusted extremists."

Drawn from local ranks

Some of the jihadis are drawn from the ranks of local militant organizations, including Al-Badr (backed by the extremist religious party Jamaat-e-Islami), the Kashmiri outfits Harakat-ul

Mujahideen and Jaish-e Mohammad, and the Sunni group Lashkar-e Jhangvi. Most of these groups have, until recently, focused their energies on Kashmir or sectarian conflicts.

The new independent splinter groups are small, receive funding from Al Qaeda, and attack Western targets using tactics like suicide bombings – once unheard of in Pakistan. Investigators in Karachi say several such groups of around 10 members each are operating in the city alone.

"They [Al Qaeda] are mostly banking on local jihadis," says one police investigator. "They themselves don't want to be seen on the ground as they don't feel safe, so they rely on these brainwashed jihadis."

To recruit, Al Qaeda leaders or operatives rely on trusted contacts, preferably people who have fought with Arabs or have been trained by them, says a senior Karachi police investigator. The go-between appoints a group of leaders, who in turn hires the services of members and assigns tasks mostly on the instructions coming from the go-between. For the jihadis, the work can be lucrative – they are paid $170 to $340 a month.

Amjad Farooqi, a top militant reportedly killed by security forces on Sunday, was a main recruiter. A veteran of the Afghan resistance in the early 1990s, he linked up with Al Qaeda operatives following Sept. 11, 2001. Security forces arrested some 10 suspected Al Qaeda-linked Pakistani militants following the interrogation of two arrested accomplices of Mr. Farooqi.

The rise of splinter groups has made the task of investigators much more difficult. The police recently recovered a booklet of instructions from a jihadi in the wake of the ongoing crackdown.

"Don't roam around with beard and Islamic dress in fashionable neighborhoods," read the instructions. "Always take out the chip of the mobile [phone] while sleeping to avoid being caught. Use mobile [phone] from a crowded place so police don't locate the positioning. Don't write the original numbers of mujahids in a notebook, try to memorize the last three digits."

To bolster secrecy, group members do not know the real names of their comrades, and only group leaders know the whereabouts of other members, says a police official. Suicide bombers are mostly young and usually live and operate separately, he adds.

'The battle is on'

The growing influence of militant groups within the law enforcement agencies has also set alarm bells ringing. Three policemen acted as suicide bombers in the Shiite mosques in Karachi and Quetta. Several low-ranking personnel from the armed forces were arrested for their alleged involvement in the foiled assassination attempts against President Pervez Musharraf.

"It is difficult to monitor the profiles of these new recruits and the new groups," says Karachi police chief Tariq Jameel. "If we want to defeat them then there is a need of collective effort from the entire society to eliminate terrorism and extremism. They are chasing us and we are chasing them. The battle is on."

(This thread was dispatched by me to twenty one individuals including president@whiethouse.gov and many organizations as a part of "The Nose of The News" on Thursday, 7 October, 2004 5:22 PM)

Dispatch: 3

President Bush's Cabinet: White House Government (February 2005)

The tradition of the Cabinet dates back to the beginnings of the Presidency itself. One of the principal purposes of the Cabinet (drawn from Article II, Section 2 of the Constitution) is to advise the President on any subject he may require relating to the duties of their respective offices.

The Cabinet includes the Vice President and the heads of 15 executive departments – the Secretaries of Agriculture, Commerce, Defense, Education, Energy, Health and Human Services, Homeland Security, Housing and Urban Development, Interior, Labor, State, Transportation, Treasury, and Veterans Affairs, and the Attorney General. Under President George W. Bush, Cabinet-level rank also has been accorded to the Administrator, Environmental Protection Agency; Director, Office of Management and Budget; the Director, National Drug Control Policy; and the U.S. Trade Representative.

Department of Agriculture

Secretary Mike Johanns

www.usda.gov

Department of the Interior

Secretary Gale Norton

www.doi.gov

Department of Commerce

Secretary Carlos Gutierrez

www.doc.gov

Department of Justice

Attorney General Alberto Gonzales

www.usdoj.gov

Department of Defense

Secretary Donald Rumsfeld

www.defenselink.mil

Department of Labor

Secretary Elaine Chao

www.dol.gov

Department of Education

Secretary Margaret Spellings

www.ed.gov

Department of State

Secretary Condoleezza Rice

www.state.gov

Department of Energy

Secretary Samuel W. Bodman

www.energy.gov

Department of Transportation

Secretary Norman Mineta

www.dot.gov

Department of Health &

Human Services

Secretary Michael O. Leavitt

www.dhhs.gov

Department of the Treasury

Secretary John Snow

www.ustreas.gov

Department of Homeland Security

Secretary Tom Ridge

www.dhs.gov

Department of Veterans Affairs

Secretary Jim Nicholson

www.va.gov

Department of Housing &

Urban Development

Secretary Alphonso Jackson

www.hud.gov

Cabinet Rank Members

The Vice President

Richard B. Cheney

www.whitehouse.gov/vicepresident/

President's Chief of Staff

Andrew H. Card, Jr.

Office of Management and Budget Director

Joshua B. Bolten

www.omb.gov

United States Trade Representative

Ambassador Robert B. Zoellick

www.ustr.gov

Office of National

Drug Control Policy

John Walters

www.whitehousedrugpolicy.gov

Presidents of United States of America (A Journey through History)

Adams, John

1797-1801

Adams, John

1825-29

Arthur, Chester

1881-85

Buchanan, James

1857-61

Bush, George H.W.

1989-93

Bush, George W.

2001-present

Carter, Jimmy

1977-81

Cleveland, Grover

1885-89, 1893-97

Clinton, William J.

1993-2001

Coolidge, Calvin

1923-29

Eisenhower, Dwight

1953-61

Fillmore, Millard

1850-53

Ford, Gerald

1974-77

Garfield, James

1881

Grant, Ulysses S.

1869-77

Harding, Warren

1921-23

Harrison, Benjamin

1889-93

Harrison, William Henry

1841

Hayes, Rutherford B.

1877-81

Hoover, Herbert

1929-33

Jackson, Andrew

1829-37

Jefferson, Thomas

1801-09

Johnson, Andrew

1865-69

Johnson, Lyndon

1963-69

Kennedy, John F.

1961-63

Lincoln, Abraham

1861-65

Madison, James

1809-17

McKinley, William

1897-1901

Monroe, James

1817-25

Nixon, Richard

1969-74

Pierce, Franklin

1853-57

Polk, James

1845-49

Reagan, Ronald

1981-89

Roosevelt, Franklin D.

1933-45

Roosevelt, Theodore

1901-09

Taft, William H.

1909-13

Taylor, Zachary

1849-50

Truman, Harry S

1945-53

Tyler, John

1841-45

Van Buren, Martin

1837-41

Washington, George

1789-97

Wilson, Woodrow

1913-21

(This thread was dispatched by me to twelve individuals including president@whiethouse.gov and many organizations as part of "The Nose of The News" on Thursday, 10 February, 2005 8:50 P

Dispatch: 4

China's Hidden Game (Excerpts from Military.com website between April-5, 2005)

On April 1, 2001, Chinese J-8 fighters intercepted a U.S. Navy VQ1 squadron surveillance aircraft, the EP-3, in the skies over the South China Sea. A mid-air collision involving one of the J-8s and the EP-3 sent the Chinese jet into the ocean and forced the U.S. plane to make an emergency landing in Chinese territory — the island of Hainan, just off the southern coast of China.

The 24 crew members of the EP-3 were eventually returned to the U.S. after being held on Chinese soil for 11 days, but other issues, including the return of the EP-3 aircraft and whether China is was appropriating its technology, turned out to be stickier.

Revisit this incident through the timeline and news articles below, and check the Media Center links to keep abreast of the latest developments involving the U.S. and China. You'll also find more background on U.S.-China relations over the years.

China Threat, Round Three

Does China's People's Liberation Army have the teeth to chomp down on Taiwan? Responding to a twitchy New York Times story from last week, China-watcher Jeffrey Lewis said no. But Jane's Defence Weekly thinks the answer may soon be yes.

An emerging consensus among long-time PLA observers, including within the US intelligence community, is that the Chinese military has successfully achieved a far-reaching qualitative advancement in its war-fighting capabilities since the beginning of this decade. The PLA is quickly becoming an increasingly credible threat against Taiwan and could even begin to pose a challenge to US military preponderance in East Asia in the next decade if the momentum is sustained.

The country's leadership has given strong backing to the PLA's transformation and force-regeneration efforts, which has translated into a hefty and sustained increase in military spending over the past few years. The officially published defence budget has risen on average by 15 per cent over the past five years from ¥121 billion ($15 billion) in 2001 to ¥220 billion last year...

The Pentagon and US intelligence community estimates that these published figures represent between one-third and one half of actual Chinese military expenditures.

The PLA is engaged in a rapid build up of necessary assets that includes amassing a sizeable short- and medium-range ballistic missile force, cruise missiles and special operations units, and strengthening its strategic surveillance, reconnaissance and targeting capabilities. The Taiwanese Defence Ministry in March 2005 reported that the PLA had deployed around 700 ballistic missiles in the vicinity of the Taiwan Strait and was also quickly building an arsenal of at least 200 Hong-Niao cruise missiles within the next year...

To be able to fight high-tech wars, the PLA is shifting its recruitment system from a reliance on poorly educated conscripts, who now serve only two years, to emphasise the development of a professional long-serving cadre of troops.... The PLA will reduce its manpower from 2.5 million to 2.3 million soldiers by the end of this year. This comes on top of a reduction of 500,000 troops in the late 1990s....

[With the troops that are left] "the PLA has shifted focus towards amphibious operations for a significant part of the ground forces", Dennis Blasko, a former US Army attaché in China, points out. This has included the reorganisation of two motorised infantry divisions in the Nanjing and Guangzhou Military Regions into amphibious infantry divisions and the transfer of another infantry division to the navy to form a second marine brigade in the late 1990s.

Blasko estimates that around a quarter of all PLA manoeuvre units, which number around 20 divisions or brigades, plus supporting artillery and air-defence units, have participated in training exercises for amphibious operations...

[Meanwhile] The PLA Navy (PLAN) is rapidly transforming itself from a coastal force into a bluewater naval power with a force modernisation drive that is unprecedented in the post-Cold War era. "The range and number of warships the Chinese navy is acquiring can be compared to the Soviet Union's race to become an ocean-going navy to rival the US in the 1970s," said a China-based foreign naval attaché.

The US intelligence community has reported that since 2001, the Chinese shipbuilding industry has produced 23 new amphibious assault ships and 13 conventional attack submarines.

The current top priority for the PLAN is the replacement of its fleet of outdated Soviet-era conventional and nuclear submarines with five new advanced models of domestically developed and imported Russian vessels...

The long-awaited Type 093 nuclear-powered attack submarine (SSN) is also close to entering into service, with the lead vessel already undergoing sea trials and expected to be accepted by the navy this year. There are reports that three hulls of this new class have already been laid...

The Type 094 nuclear-powered ballistic missile submarine, said to be an elongated version of the Type 093 and equipped with JL-2 sea-launched intercontinental ballistic missiles, is reported to have been launched last July and could be operational within the next couple of years. This is well ahead of Pentagon forecasts, which had previously estimated that the Type 094 would not enter service until towards the end of this decade.

(This thread was dispatched by me to seven individuals including president@whiethouse.gov and many organizations as part of "The Nose of The News" on Thursday, 14 April, 2005 4:40 PM)

Dispatch: 5

The Year Bypassed: The Terror and Blood

London-In the second half of the year 2005, and perhaps in the worst manner, terror hit one of the world's finest cities, London. A coordinated blast ripped through of the whole city of most civilized British people, at three different places. London was shaken. An Al-Qaeda supported terror outfit took the responsibility; investigations are still on. The Tony Blair government is thinking of strengthening its ties with its old partner the USA in the War on Terror.

July 5, 2005: The disputed pilgrim town of Ayodhya in a northern province of India suffered with one of the worst terror attacks in history ,when the 3.5 acres makeshift Ram Temple compound was attacked by five terrorists of Jaish-E-Mohammad/Lashkar-e Taiba in 3.5 acres makeshift Ram temple compound. In a two hour battle with security forces all five terrorists were gunned down.

Deepawali, 2005: A series of coordinated blasts hit India's capital, New Delhi in a crowded market. Festivity turned in to a dark night. 70 people were killed.

Baghdad: Baghdad is burning. Despite an election under the shadow of the US military the insurgents and looters kept challenging US forces in Baghdad.

Kashmir Valley- The terrorists kept bombing India's beautiful valley while getting support from across the border.

The Superescape: The Al-Qaeda boss Osama Bin Laden's next in command Abu Musab Zarkavi and Mulla Umar narrowly escaped and survived death while coming under attack by US bombardment.

Abu Salem: One of the most wanted terrorists and aid of Dawood Ibrahim, was deported by Indian investigative agency officials from Portugal. He was wanted in many killings including that of music King Gulshan Kumar and also for the Mumbai bomb blasts of January 2003.

Indian Institute of Science: Towards the last days of 2005, when most of the people were bidding farewell to 2005 a terror groups, Jaish–e-Mohammad and Lashkar-e –Taiba attacked Indian's finest institution killing two professors and four employees.

Hollywood also came under threat when Russell Crowe, a New Zealand born actor received threats from Al-Qaeda.

France: Witnessed one of the worst riots in its history when more than 5,000 motor vehicles were set on fire by rioters.

Nature's Calamity:

USA, India, Indonesia and Baluchistan all suffered with major losses due to tsunamis, hurricanes and earthquakes, which took over more than a million lives in all kind of calamities.

The Success of Science:

Amidst many terror attacks and natural calamities, sciences kept taking steady steps across the globe. NASA over came with the traumatic loss of the Colombia STAS 117 tragedy. Jet Propulsion Laboratory peeped in to the center of the universe and searched out for new solar systems and also looked for facts about the origin and expansion of the universe. TARA spacecraft looked deep in to the tsunamis of India and Indonesia, while the Cassini space craft Cassini discovered new facts and a new moon about of Saturn.

Here are few great stories from JPL:

December 6, 2005

NASA's Cassini Images Reveal Spectacular Evidence of an Active Moon

Jets of fine, icy particles streaming from Saturn's moon Enceladus were captured in recent images from NASA's Cassini spacecraft. The images provide unambiguous visual evidence that the moon is geologically active.

"For planetary explorers like us, there is little that can compare to the sighting of activity on another solar system body," said Dr. Carolyn Porco, Cassini imaging team leader at the Space Science Institute in Boulder, Colo. "This has been a heart-stopper, and surely one of our most thrilling results."

The Cassini images clearly show multiple jets emanating from the moon's south polar region. Based on earlier data, scientists strongly suspected these jets arise from warm fractures in the region. The fractures, informally dubbed "tiger stripes," are viewed essentially broadside in the new images.

The fainter, extended plume stretches at least 186 kilometers (300 miles) above the surface of Enceladus, which is only 186 kilometers wide. Cassini flew through the plume in July, when it passed a few hundred kilometers above the moon. During that flyby, Cassini's instruments measured the plume's constituent water vapor and icy particles.

Imaging team members analyzed images of Enceladus taken earlier this year at similar viewing angles. It was a rigorous effort to demonstrate that earlier apparitions of the plumes, seen as far back as January, were in fact real and not due to imperfections in the camera.

The recent images were part of a sequence planned to confirm the presence of the plumes and examine them in finer detail. Imaging team member Dr. Andrew Ingersoll from the California Institute of Technology in Pasadena, said, "I think what we're seeing are ice particles in jets of water vapor that emanate from pressurized vents. To form the particles and carry them aloft, the vapor must have a certain density, and that implies surprisingly warm temperatures for a cold body like Enceladus."

Imaging scientists are comparing the new views to earlier Cassini data in hopes of arriving at a more detailed, three-dimensional picture of the plumes and understanding how activity has come about on such a small moon. They are not sure about the precise cause of the moon's unexpected geologic vitality.

"In some ways, Enceladus resembles a huge comet," said Dr. Torrence Johnson, imaging team member from NASA's Jet Propulsion Laboratory in Pasadena. "Only, in the case of Enceladus, the energy source for the geyser-like activity is believed to be due to internal heating by perhaps radioactivity and tides rather than the sunlight which causes cometary jets." The new data also give yet another indication of how Enceladus keeps supplying material to Saturn's gossamer E ring.

November 29, 2005

NASA Rover Helps Reveal Possible Secrets of Martian Life

Life may have had a tough time getting started in the ancient environment that left its mark in the Martian rock layers examined by NASA's Opportunity rover. The most thorough analysis yet of the rover's discoveries reveals the challenges life may have faced in the harsh Martian environment.

"This is the most significant set of papers our team has published," said Dr. Steve Squyres of Cornell University, Ithaca, N.Y. He is principal investigator for the science instruments on Opportunity and its twin Mars Exploration Rover, Spirit. The lengthy reports reflect more thorough analysis of Opportunity's findings than earlier papers.

Scientists have been able to deduce that conditions in the Meridiani Planum region of Mars were strongly acidic, oxidizing, and sometimes wet. Those conditions probably posed stiff challenges to the potential origin of Martian life.

Based on Opportunity's data, nine papers by 60 researchers in volume 240, issue 1 of the journal Earth and Planetary Science Letters discuss what this part of the Martian Meridiani Planum region was like eons ago. The papers present comparisons to some harsh habitats on Earth and examine the ramifications for possible life on Mars.

Dr. Andrew Knoll of Harvard University, Cambridge, Mass., a co-author of the paper, said, "Life that had evolved in other places or earlier times on Mars, if any did, might adapt to Meridiani conditions, but the kind of chemical reactions we think were important to giving rise to life on Earth simply could not have happened at Meridiani."

Scientists analyzed data about stacked sedimentary rock layers 23 feet thick, exposed inside "Endurance Crater." They identified three divisions within the stack. The lowest, oldest portion had the signature of dry sand dunes; the middle portion had windblown sheets of sand. Particles in those two layers were produced in part by previous evaporation of liquid water. The upper portion, with some layers deposited by flowing water, corresponded to layers Opportunity found earlier inside a smaller crater near its landing site.

Materials in all three divisions were wet both before and after the layers were deposited by either wind or water. Researchers described chemical evidence that the sand grains deposited in the layers had been altered by water before the layers formed. Scientists analyzed how acidic water moving through the layers after they were in place caused changes such as the formation of hematite-rich spherules within the rocks.

Experimental and theoretical testing reinforces the interpretation of changes caused by acidic water interacting with the rock layers. "We made simulated Mars rocks in our laboratory, then infused acidic fluids through them," said researcher Nicholas Tosca from the State University of New York, Stony Brook. "Our theoretical model shows the minerals predicted to form when those fluids evaporate bear a remarkable similarity to the minerals identified in the Meridiani outcrop."

The stack of layers in Endurance Crater resulted from a changeable environment perhaps 3.5 to 4 billion years ago. The area may have looked like salt flats occasionally holding water, surrounded by dunes. The White Sands region in New Mexico bears a similar physical resemblance. For the chemistry and mineralogy of the environment, an acidic river basin named Rio Tinto, in Spain, provides useful similarities, said Dr. David Fernandez-Remolar of Spain's Centro de Astrobiologia and co-authors.

Many types of microbes live in the Rio Tinto environment, one of the reasons for concluding that ancient Meridiani could have been habitable. However, the organisms at Rio Tinto are descended from populations that live in less acidic and stressful habitats. If Meridiani had any life, it might have had to originate in a different habitat.

"You need to be very careful when you are talking about the prospect for life on Mars," Knoll said. "We've looked at only a very small parcel of Martian real estate. The geological record Opportunity has examined comes from a relatively short period out of Mars' long history."

(This thread was dispatched by me to fourteen individuals including president@whiethouse.gov and many organizations as part of "The Nose of The News" on Thursday, 12 January, 2006 8:27 PM)

Dispatch-6

The Ayodhya and Banaras Attacks: The Shadow on a Dozen More Cities

15th April, 2005

Jaunpur, a city on the railway tracks between Ayodhya and Banaras, an old heritage town of the British and the Moughals)

Place – A cyber café of one of my students in OlanGanj, by the name of Maximus.

Time –1:15 PM Indian time.

One after another a series of terrorist attacks strikes in India when it is trying to stand on its feet on a global platform and is declaring its new nuclear policies. The Indian dream of India for a big gain with a civilian nuclear deal with the United States of America has suffered with a series of terror attacks on certain soft target cities. Amazingly, it appears that this city lies within a radius of 200-300 kms on both sides of the railway track that has now been targeted. This time a wave of terror attacks has been planned on religious cities to destroy India's communal harmony. This may be due to India's increasing relations with the USA, in a Sonia Gandhi led new government

Amazingly, the attacks on the Sankat Mochak Hanuman Mandir in the holy city of Banaras, in the twin town of Ayodhya and Faizabad, in a mosque in New Delhi and in India's silicon valley, Bangalore are trying to point out that plenty of terror groups are active in India. They may be working with different/ changed names as their mother organizations have already been traced out and now they have adopted a new strategy.

India's leap in space science along with NASA, and its nuclear deal with the United States of America is are visible both on the NASA and white White House websites.

Well the terror strike in these religious cities may be seen in the light of India's will for an international collaboration with the US. The scientists and teachers at VBS Purvanchal University indicates this when I talked about the terror attacks in Ayodhya and Banaras.

The city is a heavily Muslim populous town and you may see many mosques and madarsas imparting fundamental and religious training to Muslim youths. You may see it in a broader light, but you have to think when you get to know that some of the young blood have been arrested and put behind bars on allegations of their involvement in such activities.

(This thread was dispatched by me to seven individuals including president@whiethouse.gov and many organizations as part of "The Nose of The News" on Saturday, 15 April, 2006 2:08 PM)

Dispatch – 7

(Excerpts from whitehouse.gov website)

Protecting the Homeland

President Bush's Top Priority Is The Safety And Security Of The American People. Since September 11th, President Bush has restructured and reformed the Federal government to focus resources on counterterrorism and to ensure the security of our homeland.

The Administration Has Worked With Congress To Implement The 9/11 Commission's Recommendations. Since the Commission issued its final report, the Administration has taken action on 37 of the Commission's 39 recommendations that apply to the Executive Branch and is working with Congress to continue to improve intelligence and homeland security.

Administration Officials Repeatedly Have Testified On The Implementation Of The Recommendations. Officials from the Intelligence Community, the Department of Homeland Security, the Department of Defense, the Department of State, and other agencies have testified before Congress on the recommendations of the 9/11 Commission in over 50 hearings since the Commission issued its final report.

The President Supported The Work Of The Commission. The White House provided the 9/11 Commission with unprecedented access, including providing close to 1,000 interviews with Administration officials and making available 2.3 million pages of documents for the Commission's review.

Key Institutional Developments And Accomplishments

Appointing The Director Of National Intelligence. President Bush signed into law the landmark Intelligence Reform and Terrorism Prevention Act of 2004, which overhauls the intelligence community, mandating a range of reforms and centralizing in one office key authorities. The Director of National Intelligence (DNI) serves as President Bush's principal intelligence advisor and the leader of the Intelligence Community. The first DNI, Ambassador John Negroponte, was confirmed by the Senate and sworn in this past April.

Establishing The National Counterterrorism Center (NCTC). The NCTC assists in analyzing and integrating foreign and domestic intelligence acquired from all U.S. government departments and agencies pertaining to the war on terrorism. The Center identifies, coordinates, and prioritizes the counterterrorism intelligence requirements of America's intelligence agencies and develops strategic operational plans for implementation. In July 2005, the Senate confirmed the President's nominee, Vice Admiral Scott Redd, to become the first Director of the NCTC.

Establishing The Domestic Nuclear Detection Office (DNDO). The DNDO, in the Department of Homeland Security, provides a single federal organization to develop and deploy a nuclear-detection system to thwart the importation of illegal nuclear or radiological materials.

Appointing A Privacy And Civil Liberties Oversight Board. The President has nominated the Chairman and Vice Chairman and appointed the other three members to serve on the Privacy and Civil Liberties Oversight Board, to further help ensure that privacy and civil rights are not eroded as we fight the War on Terror.

Establishing The Terrorist Screening Center. In order to consolidate terrorist watch lists and provide around-the-clock operational support for Federal and other government law-enforcement personnel across the country and around the world, the Administration created the Terrorist Screening Center. The Center ensures that government investigators, screeners, and agents are working with the same unified, comprehensive set of information about terrorists.

Transforming The FBI To Focus On Preventing Terrorism. The President has led the effort to transform the FBI into an agency focused on preventing terrorist attacks through intelligence collection and other key efforts, while improving its ability to perform its traditional role as a world-class law-enforcement agency.

Strengthening Transportation Security Through Screening And Prevention. Since 9/11 the Transportation Security Administration (TSA) has made significant advancements in aviation security, including the installation of hardened cockpit doors, a substantial increase in the number of Federal Air Marshals, the training and authorization of thousands of pilots to carry firearms in the cockpit, the 100 percent screening of all passengers and baggage, and the stationing of explosives-detection canine teams at each of the Nation's largest. These initiatives have raised the bar in aviation security and shifted the threat.

Improving Border Screening And Security Through The US-VISIT Entry-Exit System. US-VISIT uses cutting-edge biometric technology to help ensure that our borders remain open to legitimate travelers but closed to terrorists. US-VISIT is in place at 115 airports, 14 seaports, and

50 land border crossings across the country. Since January 2004, more than 39 million visitors have been checked through US-VISIT.

Establishing The National Targeting Center (NTC) To Screen All Imported Cargo. DHS established the NTC to examine cargo and passengers destined for the United States to identify those presenting the greatest threat. The NTC screens data on 100 percent of inbound shipping containers (9 million per year) to identify those posing a "high risk." CBP personnel examine 100 percent of high-risk containers.

Expanding Shipping Security Through The Container Security Initiative (CSI). The CSI is currently established in over 35 major international seaports to pre-screen shipping containers for illicit or dangerous materials before they are loaded on vessels bound for the United States.

Developing Project Bioshield To Increase Preparedness For A Chemical, Biological, Radiological, Or Nuclear Attack. Project BioShield is a comprehensive effort that will ensure that resources ($5.6 billion) are available to pay for "next-generation" medical countermeasures, expedite the conduct of NIH research and development on medical countermeasures based on the most promising recent scientific discoveries, and give FDA the ability to make promising treatments quickly available in emergency situations. Project BioShield will help protect Americans against a chemical, biological, radiological, or nuclear attack.

Cracking Down On Terrorist Financing With Our International Partners. Over 400 individuals and entities have been designated pursuant to Executive Order 13224, resulting in nearly $150 million in frozen assets and millions more blocked in transit or seized at borders. We have built an international coalition that is applying more rigorous financial standards and controls to help prevent terrorists' use of the international financial system. Specifically, we have established with the Government of Saudi Arabia a Joint Task Force on Terrorism Finance that serves as a coordinating mechanism to cooperate on important terrorism-financing investigations.

Increasing Cooperation And Reform Among International Partners At The Front Lines Of The War On Terror. In Pakistan over the next five years, we will provide more than $3 billion in security, economic, and development assistance to enhance counterterrorism capacity and promote continued reform, including of the education system. In the last three years, the United States provided more than $4.5 billion in reconstruction, economic, and security assistance programs to Afghanistan.

(This thread was dispatched by me only to president@whiethouse.gov as part of "The Nose of The News" on Wednesday, 3 May, 2006 11:46 AM

Dispatch-8

Friday, July 10, 2009

India, USA and Middle East—Changing Equations

Dear All,

We are living in a unipolar world. After the division of the former Soviet Union and its decline into a troubled economy, the world intended to lean towards the other super power, United States of America. The scenario emerged out after second world war, when the world was divided into communist and capitalist blocks this time a large number of countries started leaning towards the United States of America. The countries like France, Germany and Italy who were in the group of Axis countries and fought against the USA leaned towards America.

The USA not only helped these countries to re-strengthen their economy, but it also helped smaller countries in Africa. And in return, we all know that the CIA sought its own interest in these countries. The CIA reshuffled the govts and helped favourable governments to come in power. The USA also selected its power centers in the middle Middle East by supporting the countries like UAE, Saudi Arabia and Jordan. It also helped Israel to fight against Palestine and its so called terror organisation, Hamas. In Afghanistan, the USA initially helped the Taliban to fight out the USSR army, and succeeded in this.

This is the first half of the story, before the division of the USSR. In due course, and during the regime of Senior Bush Senior USA realised that its goal has been achieved in Afganistan, but the taliban Taliban was now is asking for its own pound of flesh, and thus wanted to rule in Afghanistan. A second threat that the US has had to face in the coming years was that of Al Qaeda, an organisation created on fanatic Islamic ideology.

Now, it is essential to know the ideology and origin of Bin Laden. Bin Laden (this includes ancestors of Osama Bin Laden), were rich businessman living in the western coast of the US. Not only this, but the Ladens were well connected with the royal family of Saudi Arabia and were having growing business with them in oil and real estate. A younger member of the Laden family, called Osama Bin Laden, had a keen tendency towards a rather rigid sect of Islam that is called Wahabism. The Wahabis restricts so many common traditions of Islam that it becomes difficult for everyday living. These Wahabis are supported by the Saudis. The liberal Islamic world and the countries which that were pro- America did not like it, but it is studied seen that religious leaders of these countries supported Osama to work on his ideology.

This was the birth of Al Qaeda.

Saddam Hussein was a dictator at large and had ruled Iraq for decades. He opposed the US on its claim of hidden biological weapons.

The September 11 attacks on the World Trade Center made America realise that it is actually on the threshold of a clear confrontation and was the target of the once sheltered Laden. Now President Bush came up with a new terminology, of "WAR ON TERROR", to fight against these evil forces and to extend its fight beyond American boundaries. In due course of time America claimed that Iraq not only had weapons of mass destruction but also had a link with Laden and Al Qaeda.

So the Bush administration, along with its old enemies and new friends, launched a heavy war fare in Iraq, and this time unlikely his father, Bush not only won the war but captured and hanged Saddam Hussein.

India, which was at one time a friend with of Iraq remained, a silent witness to this and leaned towards the US. America proposed a deal of civilian usage of nuclear energy and India welcomed it with an open heart. Experts suggest that the two countries, victimised by terror outfits, realised that it is time to shake hands and come closer.

In return India remained silent on US's stand on imposing restrictions on Iran on developing nuclear arsenals.

This is a time when neither George W Bush is in power nor Saddam Hussein is alive.

India is visiting a swift change in its foreign policy. Bin Laden is there but the Obama administration has deleted the "WAR ON TERROR" term from the dictionary of the White House. India and the US are coming closer and the global recession of 2008 is slowly getting weaker.

And in this scenario we may see new friends and new foreign policies in India, US and in the Middle East. God knows who will be on more benefitting which side in the business of war and religion.

Written by Ratnesh Dwivedi on 10.07.2009

(This thread was dispatched by me only to seven individuals and organizations including president@whiethouse.gov as part of "The Nose of The News" on Friday, 10 July, 2009 5:28 PM)

Dispatch-9

Friday, July 17, 2009

Indo-Pak Relations-Moments of Truth

India and Pakistan are on clear confrontation with each other since the Mumbai terrorist attacks. India claims and it is true it is that the Mumbai terror attacks were planned in Pakistan, and the attackers were trained inside the Pak border. Hafiz Saeed, the Jamat –ud-Dawa chief is at large in Pakistan, and India claims and has given evidences of his being the mastermind of 26/11.

The Non Aligned Movement once founded by India, Egypt and Turkey on during the peak of the cold Cold War, to remain distant with from either of the super powers, has given a platform to

Indian and Pakistani premiers to come together to think on bilateral relations. The Egypt edition of NAM in which both the sides diluted their stands, is an ice breaking step. Pakistan this time has hidden the Kashmir issue, while India only mentioned about the Pakistani action on the Mumbai accused. The Indian Prime Minister would be in Delhi when I am writing these lines.

The history of India- Pakistan relations has been a saga of truth, accusation, infiltration, terrorism, occupation and betrayal. So far, India and Pakistan haves come into clear confrontation that led to a war, for four times. But there haves been remarkable steps as well to re-strengthen the relations between the two neighbours.

THE BITTER MOMENTS

On the strategic will of British rule and Mohammad Ali Zinnah, Pakistan came into existence in 1947, and couple of months later Pakistan infiltrated Pashtun tribes with the help of the Pakistani army into the Kashmir. The then Maharaja of Kashmir Hari Singh sought Indian help to fight out the infiltration and India asked to him to sign an accord to be an integral part of India. Seeing no way to of escape Hari Singh signed the deal and in return Indian troops defeated Pakistani infiltration.

In 1965, under the leadership of Lal Bahadur Shashtri India fought another war with Pakistan, and the Indian army reached as close as up to 18 kms from Lahore. The USSR mediated in for a ceasefire agreement that was signed in Tashkant. Experts say that Lal Bahadur Shastri could not stand up to the international pressure and died of a heart attack.

1971 saw another war between India and Pakistan on both sides of the border, when Shiekhs Mujjebur Rehman seeked sought Indian help to liberate East Pakistan from the traumatic leadership of integral Pakistan. India's then Prime Minister Indira Gandhi helped Bangladesh Mukti Vahini and succeeded in liberating Bangladesh. The war was fought along the eastern and western borders.

Between 1972 and 1999 there haves been many issues including that of terrorism and Kashmir which have lead India and Pakistan to a clear confrontation.

In 1999 we saw the Kargil war in the back drop of the Lahore talks.

And most recently 26/11 happened which was again a cowardly act by Pakistan based militant groups, in the line of with many other attacks in Indian cities.

BETTER MOMENTS

Despite many turbulences and confrontations, full scale war and war like situations, there haves been moments when India and Pakistan sat together for betterment of relations and friendly ties.

Simla Agreement 1972 – First time India and Pakistan came together under the premiership of Zulfikar Ali Bhutto and Indira Gandhi. Issues like intrusion and Kashmir were discussed and the Simla pact was signed.

In the 1988 the then prime ministers of India and Pakistan, Rajiv Gandhi and Benazir Bhutto talked about not interrupting the nuclear programmes of any country.

1998, visited Lahore talks when Indian prime minister Mr Vajpayee and Nawaz Sharif talked about opening diplomatic relations, starting a bus service and the Kashmir issue.

In 2003 again Vajpayee and Musharraf came together in the Agra summit, which was another ice breaking step after the Kargil war.

So the history of Indo Pak relation has been a story of magical and miserable moments . It also has been a story of trust and betrayal. India has always welcomed Pakistan for talks but not on the conditions of Internationalization of the Kashmir issue. On the other hand Pakistan has always has tried US interference in the Kashmir dispute.

For the first time US President Barack Obama is unwilling to interfere in the bilateral talks and wishes that the issue is actually an internal matter of India and Pakistan.

Again India and Pakistan are coming close and we have to see if a new chapter of friendship and warmth will be written or it would one more step towards false promises and assurance and betrayal. Two good neighbours are sharing the one grilling pain of terrorism or two old enemies are sharpening their weapons to stab each other; whether two emerging economies of South Asia wish to talk their domestic problems in the time of recession or two economies are troubling the common public by imposing disturbances, terrorism and war or war like situations.

The world is watching through the international media what is going to happen next in South Asian relations, a history written by the ink of friendship and trust or a chapter unfolding another war between two nuclear states.

Let us watch...

Written by Ratnesh Dwivedi on 17/07/09

(This thread was dispatched by me only to seventeen individuals and organizations including president@whiethouse.gov as part of "The Nose of The News" on Friday, 17 July, 2009 6:00 PM)

Dispatch-10

To,

Barack Obama

Honourable President of United States of America

White House Govt

White House

Washington D.C.

Sub- In the name of Peace and Prosperity. (Referring President's Oslo Speech)

Honourable Sir,

Not too long ago when the world witnessed horrible terror attacks on American soil, to whom the media refers to as 9/11. Perhaps this incident was the beginning of Al Qaeda's bloody foot print in the civilised world. It was not the first terror attack on American soil or people, or elsewhere in the world, but it was perhaps the beginning of a rare kind of war against human civilization. World Wars were as dangerous and the Cold War era was even more, but the religion adopted by these people to whom we refer as "terrorists" perhaps have given birth to an unending war against human institutions. We hardly see any sign that these animals and their religion is going to accept the idea of democracy and the idea of peace.

Mahatma Gandhi and Martin Luther King were great men s of all time, and the path they made for humanity and brotherhood is a rare kind of example that must be adopted by one and all. But as you spoke out in your historical speech that there comes a time when the ideas and paths of people like Gandhi and King becomes a little irrelevant. In the a time when humanity and the concept of democracy is are in danger not only in the United States of America but also across the globe and in countries like India , we cannot sit together and look towards Gandhi and King for their advices. Rather, we should stand united in the name of humanity, peace and prosperity, for our generations to come and take an oath to defeat the idea of terrorism and extremism.

What I have understood in the last few years when I started writing to the White House govt that these people who claim to be fighting a "holy war" in the name of 'God' and '"Allah',," have enlarged their organisations across the globe and haves garnered the support of many other outfits to come together to declare a big war against humanity and civilization. They do not want to see a common people living in peace and thinking about good livelihoods for their children. They do not believe that good democracies should talk to each other to solve the problems of humanity and planet earth. They fight for their own cause and a different kind of religion which claims only lives and leaves blood on the streets.

Mr President, I believe that each all countries and individuals have the right to think of its their betterment and prosperity of their people, and have a the right to protect its their own territories f it is attacked by these people to whom we refer as "terrorist"; and in order to do that a country have has all the right to talk to other heads of states to think about how to defeat these forces.

Terrorism is not a word which is restricted to the United States of America or the Republic of India, but it is a global war today. If one country thinks that the USA is suffering, hence, let it fight alone, then perhaps it is daydreaming. Today it is USA or India, another day it would be your country and your people. It is a global war of a different kind, and no territorry and nation is safe; even the nations which are sheltering these animals, because these animal do not believe in the idea of nations or the idea of democracy.

Let us understand and think and come out with an idea on how to defeat them. It is not a fight the USA should alone tackle. It is a fight of each and every individual. A fight of each and every nation and a fight of each and every member of the human institution and a fight of each and every member of and followers of the religion of humanity. So we must stand together and must take an oath in the name of peace and humanity that we will support and protect the idea of democracy and the idea of human institution, and will defeat these animals and their religion, to whom we refer as "Terrorists", by all means and methods. This is the time and this is the moment when we all across all continents should come out to protect our planet and to save humanity from these animals because we are in a "Danger".

(This thread was dispatched by me only to five individuals and organizations including president@whiethouse.gov as part of "The Nose of The News" on Saturday, 12 December, 2009 12:38 PM)

Dispatch-11

An Open Letter to President Obama

To,

Barack H. Obama

Honourable President of United States of America

White House Govt

White House

Pensylvania Avenue

Washington D.C.

Washington

20502

And his Three Senior Advisors

David Axelrod, Vallerie Zerrot and Peter Rouse

Sub.–In response to grounding up of NASA'a Lunar Mission.

Honourable Sir,

I am Ratnesh Dwivedi in India a regular recipient of NASA's updates. But before I write anything on NASA or its missions, I would like to tell you a little about my knowledge on science research work in USA. The first American President who talked against racism was Abraham Lincoln. He was the one who seriously guided America on sciences through his mission to establish the world's biggest and most respected research organisation–The National Academy of Sciences. The National Academy of Sciences is the most respected name and a person feels high amounts of pride even if he even talks to a receptionist of NASA in Washington. So far its worthy scientists haves been honoured with dozens of Nobel prizes and other laurels. In due course of time the Academy enlarged its operations and established a few other divisions like National Research Council, Institute of Medicine and Institute of Engineering, under its umbrella.

The world's biggest space science research organisation, National Aeronautics of Space Administration (NASA) also got its association with the Academy and National Research Council launched one of its one of the rarest kind of Research Associateship Programme (RAP) to select unpanelled research scientists from across the globe to associate them with the National Academy of Sciences and with NASA through this programme. Budding scientists from countries like India got a chance to associate themselves with NASA and other disciplines of sciences and engineering. It was a remarkable step of the Academy to allow them to work on the minutest areas of life sciences, biology, biotech, engineering, technology and space sciences.

I, by that time, had collected some original research work on space sciences with the help of the information I received through NASA newsletters. I compiled it and sent the 1500 pages of research work on Space Dynamics to Mary D Cox, an official with The National Academy of Sciences. I quickly got a reply that my work has been forwarded to a NASA coordinator.

Leaving this story behind, I have always felt a significant amount of pride to learn from NASA letters and to remain in touch with NASA officials. In a recent e-mail from Whitney Calvin of Media Relation Department of Jet Propulsion Laboratory (most respected division of NASA), I got to know about some of the most optimistic missions of NASA. And the information was about designing two mega spaceships – The Aries and The Orion, which may carry a Human Voyage to the Moon and Mars, by 2020.

It may be a giant leap of human kind to touch down on the surface of the Moon once more and on the Red Planet for the first time. Mars, as I predict, is our hope to establish a Human colony in the future.

Honourable Sir, I am writing this letter in great depression that now your government have decided to wind up these missions. It is a great loss to sciences and to human kind. It is a rare chance to give an opportunity to humans to explore our solar system and to our moon and to the Red Planet. Sir, I , who have a great amount of interest in Space Sciences and in NASA activity humbly request you to allow NASA with its Lunar and Red Planet missions and to allow its scientists to carry on with the Aries and Orion spaceship programmes.

Sciences, Human kind and our generations would be obliged to the Obama administrations for ages if you live up the dreams of thousands of people like me and people in NASA by not stopping these, rarest of its kind, missions.

Thanking You.

Ratnesh Dwivedi

Dispatch-12

Death of a Professor, of a Whistle Blower

When I was travelling to my home town of Ayodhya, a rather calm pilgrim town in the northern Indian province of eastern Uttar Pradesh, I had several things on my mind, and one of these things was to meet a Professor in Awadh University – a state university in the town. But I was did not knowing that destiny has written a cruel chapter for this meeting, as this time it was not going to be possible as in my earlier visits.

Professor Vijay Kumar Pande a historian in his own right and an archaeologist, was one of the most experienced professors in the state. He had been in academics for several decades, had written several books on the historical importance of Ayodhya and Faizabad. He had led a team of students to excavate several sites of historical importance in the region and had guided dozen of students for Ph.D programme.

But somewhere in his conscious mind he was not satisfied with several people in the University, with the system of working and the many restrictions imposed upon him by some of his colleagues.

I remember my first meeting with him when I was assisting a French film maker for a documentary on Ayodhya and its cultural importance. He was a great person. Always ready to help, always ready to meet and always ready to speak. My second meeting with him was when I decided to spend a couple of years in my hometown. I went straight to him and asked him to give me an opportunity for some guest lectures. And he trusted on me for this in 2005. I stayed with him for six months without asking for payment. He never imposed his seniority over me but humbly asked me to translate one of his books into English. I started the work but it remained incomplete.

We rather spent more time in discussing academic issues, .problems in the University and the atmosphere created against him. He never feared naming out the people who restricted him from doing some good historical and archaeological work. The chief proctor of the University, as he named many times before me, had been trying to defame his reputation and restricting his research work.

I remember how depressed he was when his years long work to establish an archaeological museum was restricted into just one room store of some stones. Not only this, but Mr Proctor also was involved in beating a man who was appointed by him to guard the museum.

He was under tremendous pressure by these people as none of his projects was getting approved. He was finding himself lonely and he complained many times about this with his fellow colleagues and even to me.

He also narrated once how brutally he was beaten up by some 'gundas' on the behest of the 'Thakur' lobby of the university, some twenty odd years back.

But I can remember that the Professor was fearless. I remember, I was sitting with him late night the day Ayodhya was attacked by terrorists. He had a diary with him, perhaps a Govt Of India PRO diary, from which he searched out the Home Minister Mr Shiv Raj Patil's telephone number and straight away ranged him up and narrated the whole situation in the tensed town, for half an hour.

I remember him as my guru who taught me the ABC of Indian and World history in a couple of months. I can't forget his last phone call to me when he said, "I am very tense. Please help me out. I want to come to Delhi."

Couple of months later he met with an accident and came to Delhi for an operation and returned to Ayodhya only after his death on the operation table.

I am writing these lines but still I am thinking what tension that professor was having with him or what irregularities he was willing to point out in Awadh University,... or what threat he was having from the people he mentioned in his conversations. May be his worries require an attention by the academia and media. May god rest him in peace.

Written by Ratnesh Dwivedi

(This thread was dispatched by me to eleven individuals including Rajdeep Sardesai and organization as part of "The Nose of The News" on Tuesday, 15 June, 2010 9:07 PM.)

Dispatch-13

Story of a Dying Unit: A Brain Child of Indira Gandhi

To,

The Prime Minister of India

Mrs Sonia Gandhi (UPA Chairperson)

Mr Rahul Gandhi (General Secretary – AICC)

(Through three of my best friends in Media)

Sub– Story of a dying unit–A brain child of Indira Gandhi.

Respected Sir,

I have never been in the practice to write an open letter to the three top political leaders and policy makers in India. However, my e-mail suggestions to Wwhite house House government has been appreciated -,the a practice which I am doing since 2004.

But, something inside my conscious pushed me up to write me this letter to the Prime Minister, UPA Chairperson and Mr Rahul Gandhi. I am calling him by name since I find in him a trustworthy friend and a hope of the future.

I have spent my 25 years in the area which is known as eastern Uttar Pradesh, in the district of Faizabad. I know it as a place where I have seen some of the best and worst moments of my life. Let us not go in to that.

Mankapur, a small town some 56 kms away from Faizabad and almost at the same distance from its district HQ Gonda, has been home to one of the units which brought the Telecommunication revolution in India. Indian Telephone Industries, as it is named by the Government of India, is a brain child of Mrs Indira Gandhi. Apart from its Naini Unit and Raibareli Unit, Mankarpur is blessed to have one unit of ITI at a place which falls on the railway route from Lucknow to Gorakhpur.

So, we may call it as a home and place of worship place for thousands of workers and officers who work day and night to give us equipment and technology so we may speak to our loved ones. Indian Telephone Industries has designed some of the latest technology and equipment which are at par with international standards, and the Mankapur Unit is a part of it.

The other unit or the HQ is in Bangalore.

I have been visiting the ITI Mankapur campus while I was studying in the 12th standard as one of my relatives served as an engineer in that unit. However, another reason was to enjoy the small journey through the jungle of Tikri. I guess I would have visited ITI Mankapur as many as 70 times. Hence, I have an emotional attachment with this pride of India, hence here is the story.

I can tell you with all my honesty that the ITI unit of Mankapur is a mini India. It is the bread and butter of thousands of workers and officers working inside it and also the bread and butter for several thousands of villagers and people who are indirectly dependent on the success of this unit. But now there is a danger on for these several thousands of these people and on this unit. Insiders suggest that the unit may be closed at any given point of time. The reason it is not making profit is it is under huge debt. Salaries haves not been distributed to hundreds of employees and if you talk to any of worker, officer or neighbourhood people you may examine the amount of depression they are going through.

So the brain child of Indira Gandhi is in ICU, and doctors from the places like ALCATEL (France), which tried to save it once have given up the hope.

The Big Question before these several thousands of people is how to survive?

Mrs Sonia Gandhi, once, consoled the unit with 1,000 crore rupees, but insiders suggests that it has been randomly distributed among high officials and there have been irregularities in investment of that amount.

Now the question is how to make this unit overcome with all these kind of challenges?

The Unit is dying and so are its workers and officers.

The sources suggests that only direct interference from the center may give any solution, so relying on that sources I am directing this letter to three of my friends in the Media ,in the hope that the message would be conveyed to the right people.

Regards.

Ratnesh Dwivedi

(This thread was dispatched by me to Rajdeep Sardesai as part of "The Nose of The News" on Thursday, 5 August, 2010 9:35 PM.)

Dispatch -14

The Judgement Day and Ayodhya as it Stands

by Ratnesh Dwivedi on Friday, October 1, 2010 at 5:44pm

I was in class 12 when, on Dec 6, 1992 the disputed structure was demolished by Kar Sevaks, which led to communal riots across the country. But now we all can proudly can claim that India and Indians have moved ahead, rather haves grown up mature from these unstructured sentiments. As Mr Madhukar Upadhyaya (Historian and Journalist) suggests that we cannot demolish the understanding of co- existence of Hindus and Muslims in four hours for those who are living together for thousands of years.

I have seen Ayodhya in the last thirty years growing rather in as a mature town where people do worship Lord Rama, but they also do bother about their economic standing in society, worries about the future of their kids and respect the sentiments of other communities. Ayodhya is home to Lord Rama, and other gods of Jainism, Buddhism, Sikhism, and Islam. What so ever the misunderstanding has been created between communities has been washed up. And Ayodhya reacts with full maturity to not only issues of Dharma and Rama, but to other national and international issues.

I remember when I decided to take a leave from my engagements and then to stay in my home town – Ayodhya for a couple of years, I was asked by a university professor to take some lectures in Dr RML Awadh University. I decided to speak on Space Science and I proudly can say that the students of Ayodhya were very keen to understand about this area about which most of the genius students where many bother to take care of. Even I found a little student of twelve years in the school where from I passed out from in 1992–Maharaj Intermediate College, asking me finer points of gravity and planetary systems.

So, Ayodhya has grown up and so has their beliefs in Lord Rama and the Islam.

This land mark verdict and reactions after this at least suggests it.

Now we all know that the honourable High Court suggests that the total land area of almost 70 acres shall be equally divided in three parts, while the main worship place to which the Hindus refer to as 'Garbh Griha', will stand with the Hindus.

I guess the learned judges of the Lucknow bench of the Allahabad High Court haves given a chance to both the communities to show the world that they stand together, their beliefs stand together, the people of Ayodhya and Ayodhya itself stand as one, and so is our nation –India.

This is an opportunity to show the world that the place which created such ideological, political, religious and social differences across the country may again can show the world that Ayodhya also can also give the lesson of national integrity and Universal brotherhood by constructing a huge mosque and a magnificent temple at one place where from the worshipers of Imam-e-Hind lord Lord Rama and Prophet Mohammad may show the world that we all are one.

(This thread was dispatched by me to nineteen individuals including president@whitehouse.gov as part of "The Nose of The News" on Friday, 1 October, 2010 5:54 PM. And this was my last dispatch as part of the series.)

Dispatch 15

Ayodhya and Faizabad: Moving ahead from Ram and Allah

by Ratnesh Dwivedi on Wednesday, December 29, 2010 at 12:31pm

This time when I started a trip to my home town in Ayodhya and Faizabad, I was travelling with the shadow of the Ayodhya verdict and a low intensity blast that was a fallout of the Ayodhya issue. Ayodhya and Faizabad, the twin towns are located at some 125 kms from state capital Lucknow, and are known for Ganga Jamuni tehjeeb since ages. Ayodhya, a small Hindu pilgrim town is known as the birth place of Hindu's holy god Rama, a seventh incarnation of lord Vishnu, and is one of the oldest cities of Hindu Mythology. Some 3000 temples are here as it is popularly called said that there is a temple in each house and there is a house in each temple. The temples of Ayodhya are manged by Akharas–Nirmohi, Nirvani and etc. Most of the Sadhus are Vaishnav, that means they worship Lord Vishnu.

This time when I tried to touch the pulse of common Ayodhya Vasi, interestingly no one showed any interest in the Ayodhya issue, rather they talked about the opportunities and development of the town.

Coming to Faizabad, one can profoundly say that its one of the most beautifully built (only ruins are there) cities. Once the capital of 'Awadh' in Nawab Asfuddaula's period (which was later shifted to Lucknow) it is a Muslim populated city and the Hindus too live in newly built colonies. You can see Burqa clad women in rickshaws in chowk area. Faizabad itself has some 100 old mosques and is currently visiting growth.

HDFC, ICICI and other MNC banks have opened its their branches here and all the flyovers on link bypass between/w Lucknow and Gorakhpur are operational now. The University in the city is visiting 'Winter Break' and has now has a facelift.

However, there is an opinion among the Hindus that a Ram Temple must be built. The bank of the Saryu River is empty as there is no Mela season and so are the temples.

I also interacted with some Muslim girls on their way to school; they too feel that now it's time for change and Faizabad and Ayodhya should be seen as a paradigm of change and growth and not only a place which created so much distance between the two communities.

As for as the rural population in the district is concerned, it is time to send the sugarcane crop to sugar mills and farmers are busy to shifting their crop to mills as soon as possible. One can see trucks and tractors loaded with sugar cane on its way to mills in Faizabad and Gonda. Eastern U.P produces the maximum of the total sugarcane in India.

There is a shift in the mood of Hindus and Muslims for a new chapter with religious harmony and eagerness for change and growth. The Member of Parliament from Faizabad, Nirmal Khattri should also be given credit for this change.

(This thread was dispatched by me to AP as part of "The Nose of The News" on Wednesday, 29 December, 2010 12:34 PM. And this was my last dispatch as part of the series.)

MM photo

The Teaching Assignment and Shiny Rachel Thomos

Designing "The Nose of The News" required time, study and money. I dedicated my time to reading books, searching websites and conceptualizing the episodes. I was somehow feeling busy, however it was not recognized till then. Sometimes I spent the whole day in a cyber café in Thipsandara market in search of news related stuff on the internet. But it was where I had to put all the money which I got from my brothers and parents. Dispatching it to top individuals and organizations always had the risk of questioning what was the intention behind it. But I did not stop and kept e-mailing the dispatches every week, mostly on Thursdays. I carried "The Nose of The News" until I was not fully engaged in a permanent full time job in 2008. This was the longest piece of journalistic work which I feel did not get any recognition.

There was a requirement for money if I had to carry my passion of writing reports and dispatching them. Sometimes I had to pay a whole day's surfing charges to the cyber café in Thipsandara. Let me confess that at times I even stole some money to fulfil my obsession. But soon I realized that if I required to carry this forward I had to get a job. Soon, on other days of the week I started roaming around the city for a media job. But it was not my luck. I shifted my search from industry to academics as I had some experience of teaching in a media school. Bangalore is not as big as Delhi, so I could roam in each corner of the city in one day. It had also got almost seventy colleges which were running journalism programs. Some of these colleges were private, having AICTE and affiliation with Bangalore University.

One fine morning I saw an advertisement in my newspaper which was about a teaching assignment in a private college running a journalism program at bachelors level. I thought to try my luck and called the given number.

St George College of Management and Science was one of those colleges in Bangalore which somehow managed to get affiliation of AICTE and Bangalore University. It was run in a small building painted in white. The owner of the college was a shrewd businessman. He understood that I was in need of a job and would agree on his terms and conditions; he called me to meet him. The college was located in the Basavanguddi area and was five kilometers away from my house. As soon as I reached the college I developed the fear of rejection as it had happened with me in Delhi. But as I said, the owner of the college was a shrewd man. As he became conversant about my qualifications and experience, he asked me to join from next week and asked the HR people to release my appointment letter with a salary of 7000/- a month.

When I got the appointment letter in my hands I examined it many times. My hands were trembling as if I had got something very hot in my hands. I could not believe that I had something with me for which I had waited for years. A regular job and clear-cut bifercation of my salary. It was a dream which came true. I reached my house and told my parents and then my elder brother on his return from the office. All were happy and so was I as I had a source to carry out my dream to dispatch "The Nose of The News". This was August 2004.

The Department of Journalism at St George College of Management and Science was in its first starting year and I was the only one to manage the department. But to my astonishment there were only two students to start with. One a Bengali student while the other was an Oriya. Both had come to Bangalore as they were not able to get in to their first choice of Engineering. On my first day when I was told about my duties I was also told to increase the strength of the department. I had to teach all five subjects incorporated in the first semester, which were Introduction to Mass Communication, Reporting, Basic of Editing, Audio Visual Journalism and Computer Application. Two other subjects which were part of the syllabus were taught by another faculty. There was no teacher who could teach English to the class of two students. And I started my class with my favorite subject of reporting. I had to take five continuous classes before sending both students to the computer lab, while I waited for an English faculty to join the college.

My primary concern was to motivate both students who were low on morale. I would tell them the challenges in reporting through the experience I had gained in Ayodhya and by meeting biggies in media like Rajdeep, Ami, Shikha Trivedi and Anita Pratap. To boost their morale level I would tell them how lucrative the media profession is.

One fine day I was called by the owner of the college and he told me that a new English faculty was going to join soon. In the meantime I took some advance money to dispatch episodes of "The Nose of the News".

We had one day off on Sundays . One Monday when I went to my seat I saw a lady in her thirties sitting in front of me. Shiny Rachel Thomos was from Kerla but unlike most of the Kerelaits, she had a fair complexion and pleasant personality. She was warm enough to be affectionate to everyone. I liked that I now had company with me. We talked about the timetable and courses which she was going to share with me. She was in the college to teach English.

Shiny Rachel Thomos had a little daughter in her family and her husband was in UAE. Sometimes she would carry her daughter with her. The daughter was a copy of her mother; she would stick to her the whole day and seldom go out to have a packet of chips from the nearby shop. Shiny Rachel Thomos was good at communication and I found that she was happy to share her feelings with me. I too was appreciative towards her and we both put our best efforts to run the department.

I always sat next to her to discuss the many issues related to the department and she would always come up with a solution. Our chemistry was good, our bonding was best.

I narrated that the morale of both the students was low as they did not have enough students in the class. They always worried about the legality of the college and always came to me asking if the degree was valid and recognized. I had no answer for them and always said that everything was right. One day the Bengali students came to me and told me that he was withdrawing from college and shifting to another good college where he had secured admission. It was a shock for me as I had to worry for my job. If there would not be any students, why would the shrewd owner keep me and give me a salary, I thought. Despite the best of mine and Shiny Rachel Thomos' efforts we could not hold the Bengali student and soon we found that the Oriya student also followed in the footsteps of the Bengali student.

As I had predicted, it was a waste of money to keep me in the department on the owner's part. So one day when college was about to close for the day, the owner called me and asked me to put in my papers. I was in shock and told Shiny Rahel Thomos. I had to leave a job for which I had waited and a good friend in whom I trusted.

This was the end of my two month teaching assignment as lecturer at St George College of Management and Science.

I was again jobless, I was again shattered. This was September 2004 when I started working again on my concept of "The Nose of the News" from the same cyber café in Thipsandara market.

While working on the concept of dispatches I searched for a new hobby and that was to peep in to the websites of NASA and National Academy of Sciences. This was a new world for me, a new passion which sometimes kept me in the cyber café for the whole day. I somehow got associated with the Saturn Observation Campaign, an effort of Cassini Hyugence Mission of Jet Propulsion Laboratory-NASA and came in touch with Senior Outreach Specialist Jane Huston Jones. A very optimistic mission sent to study planet Saturn and its fabulous ring and moons.

My dispatches, which I sent also to the BBC, encouraged me to speak to the people there. I was sending my e-mails to Nik Gowing at BBC in London and wanted to speak to him. So one day I just rang him up and asked if he was receiving my e-mails. Nik Gowing, a prime time anchor and editor with BBC World was educated at the Simon Langton Grammar School in Canterbury and Latymer Upper School in London, followed by the University of Bristol.

A foreign affairs specialist and presenter at ITN from 1978, Gowing became Diplomatic Editor for the flagship Channel 4 News from 1989. During his time with the BBC, Gowing has since presented The World Today (1996–2000), Europe Direct, HARDtalk, Dateline London, as well as Simpson's World.

At the time of the death of Princess Diana in 1997, Gowing anchored coverage for over seven hours, reportedly only having had 40 minutes sleep before being driven back to Television Centre to present. BBC World was being simulcast for the first time ever with the BBC domestic channel BBC One, making up a global audience of around half a billion, to whom he announced her death.

His coverage of the aftermath of the September 11th 2001 attacks won the 2002 Hotbird Award. He had been on air for six hours. He is also a Member of Council of the Royal United Services Institute.

He said that he was receiving hundreds of e-mails on a daily basis and was unable to recognize my e-mail out of the chunk. Whatever, he recognized it or deleted it from his system I admired him for the kind of coverage he did on Princess Diana's death and 9/11.

Departing to Ayodhya again

I cursed my luck which was snatching away all the opportunities time was giving me and that is all I could do after I was out from the college. I calculated that it had been a good five years that I had not been able to find a regular job and was somehow keeping engaged in so called freelancing work and designing and dispatching of "The Nose of The News". Time had given me a bad taste, destiny had written a tough chapter for me. All I could do was to accept god's will and thanked him for all the support my brother's family and parents were giving me. But as I said there is an end to everything. Somehow I realized that my brother himself was worried and upset for my non-performance or luck.

When we all realized that nothing was coming my way and as per Hindu tradition I also required to be married, my elder brother proposed a plan. For five years he had sheltered me and I had no doubt about his love and affection for me but he had responsibilities for his family as well. It is not that he was not pained and disturbed and so were my parents, but he was more worried for my future. Time was passing by very fast and social responsibilities had to be worn, so he suggested I move to my native place for a couple of years. He thought I would have to change my life, have a new atmosphere. As was tradition in my family I would get married in a cultured and civilized Brahmin family. I, who was rigid and firm that I would defeat my luck, did not like the plan initially, but had to accept it, as it was god's will.

So, towards the beginning of November 2004, I along with my parents boarded a train to my native place where I had grown up, educated and learnt a lot about media. This was a second farewell for me against my will and desire from another city. I cried when I had to leave Delhi, but I was depressed when I was deported from Bangalore. Destiny had something else for me, time had otherwise.

I was unable to react when we all reached Ayodhya. We all had not been to our village for several years. It was locked, dirty and looked like it was desperately waiting for us to arrive. It took us one week to clean our part of the house (as I had narrated earlier, our village house was the residence of my father and his two brothers and their families) and it took me one full year to finally adjust in an atmosphere which was abandoned by me and seldom visited.

For the first week I did not go anywhere and remained confined to my house. As I started moving outside my village and kept going to Ayodhya to my uncle's house I started finding new friends, those who recognized my work in 2002 and 2003 and those who had studied with me in school and college. Soon I realized that my point of depression was worth less and there was lots of life in town. I had some experience of teaching, I had experience of dispatching reports and designing my optimistic e-mail based program "The Nose of the News", and I had several months of knowledge of space science which I got during my web surfing of NASA websites in the cyber café in Thipsandara. This was the time when I must explore new avenues where opportunities were less but the people were good.

Exploring such ideas, one day I knocked at the door of a University professor.

Avadh university was rechristened as Dr. Ram Manohar Lohia Avadh University in memoriam of late Dr. Ram Manohar Lohia, an epic socio-economic ideologue and freedom fighter par excellence. The government of Uttar Pradesh established University as sheer an affiliating university. The university assumed the shape of a residential University in the year 1984. In the ab initio the residential segment became functional with the opening of the four departments in the campus viz. history, Culture and Archaeology, Rural Economics, Mathematics and Statistics and Solid State Physics.

Being adhered to the dictum 'slow and steady wins the race', this university had been incessantly growing. Under the prolific and peerless leadership of visionaries and Vice-Chancellors the work-culture of the university had witnessed a phenomenal and revolutionary change. It is under his leadership of revolutionaries and visionaries that the old dictum about work-culture had been altogether replaced by the dictum, 'Fast and forthwith progress of the university' in its every walk of life. At campus level the University had been conducting Under Graduate / Post Graduate studies and researches in the disciplines of Economics, Mathematics & Statistics, Bio-Chemistry, Microbiology, Environmental Sciences and M.B.A. Besides, the subjects of Extension Education & Rural Development, Mass Communication & Journalism, M.S.W., and Library Science and Bachelor of Technology (B.Tech.). To give an added fillip and to strengthen the residential set up a variety of courses in the umpteen disciplines of Under Graduate and Post Graduate studies were being launched in the campus in the academic session 2005-06.

Affiliated colleges spread over the 9 districts of Faizabad, Sultanpur, Pratapgarh, Ambedkarnagar, Barabanki, Balrampur, Baharaich, Shravasti and Gonda also add to the magnitude and strength of the University. The successful conduction of academic activities, continuous endeavor for quality improvement, commitment towards perfection and excellence in the University would, beyond doubt, turn this University into one of the leading Universities of the nation.

Professor Vijay Kumar Pandey, a historian in his own right and an articulate person, was the one with whom I met first in the University. He was dean of the Faculty of Arts and Head of the Department with History and Archaeology departments. He himself was an archaeologist and had excavated many sites of historical importance in nearby areas.

I met him at his residence in the professor's colony. He was living with his rather young wife. He was not blessed with children. When I was making a documentary with French filmmaker Dominique Deluzel took Dominique to meet Professor Pandey. He recalled that meeting and asked me for a copy of the documentary. And as I told him how cynical Dominique was and narrated how I was involved in designing "The Nose of the News", lecturing assignments and web search on space exploration, he randomly asked me to teach the need importance of Archaeology in the Space Science.

I was amazed at his intelligence. When most scientists believe that Space Science was purely a subject of science, the man in front of me was talking about the core and very basic thing which all space missions (manned or unmanned) do when they reach a lunar surface or another planet (in case of unmanned missions NASA had launched to various planets).

I decided to take this challenge. A person of such a great eminence had trusted me and I never wanted to betray him. This was a new concept, a challenging topic to tell the minute things of importance of Archaeology in Space Science and more over we had developed a bond where I have shared many a things with him including about that little dark but tall girl with whom I had expressed my lov in Ddelhi and who still deep inside my conscience.He asked me to go to Delhi and find here and I decided to do so.Actually I promised him to do so.

So in February 2005 I started my unwritten association with the Professor and the University for which I was rarely paid and which lasted until the next year when I got a contract for lectureship in another University in the same region.

Lectures on Space Exploration

I planned my lectures pretty well keeping the need of M.A. and Ph.D students in mind. I was going to teach such a senior class and nothing should be missed. I prepared a document which dealt with the Art of Science, about missions in Space Science by NASA, about comets which are studied through the eyes of an Archaeologist and I took a case study of a very famous and experimental mission of NASA –The Deep Impact Mission which was destined to collide with a comet Tempel-1 in May June 2005. I also discussed with the curious lot of students about the Tsunami which had made a disastrous impact in coastal India.

For a full one year I delivered these lectures with Professor Pandey's students, with students of the Engineering college of the University and with several other departments on the recommendation of professor Professor Pandey. Here are excerpts from what I discussed with the senior students of the University and how I designed it this by exploring NASA webpages and library.

Art of Science-

Thousands of years ago, on a small rocky planet orbiting a modest star in an ordinary spiral galaxy, our remote ancestors looked up and wondered about their place between Earth and sky. Today, we ask the same profound questions:

- How did the universe begin and evolve?
- How did we get here?
- Where are we going?
- Are we alone?

Today, after only the blink of an eye in cosmic time, we are beginning to answer these questions. Space probes and space observatories have played a central role in this process of discovery.

Our missions and research generate most of the coolest news coming out of NASA. We are responsible for all of NASA's programs relating to astronomy, the solar system, and the sun and its interaction with Earth. Our science stretches from the middle levels of Earth's atmosphere to the beginning of the universe, billions of light years away.

Our website serves our science community, educators, government decision-makers, and the public. We hope your visit is enjoyable. Thanks for stopping by!

Future Space Programs-

NASA's Science Goals

The 2010 Science Mission Directorate Science Plan states that NASA's goal in Planetary Science is to "ascertain the content, origin, and evolution of the solar system, and the potential for life elsewhere."

NASA missions pursue this goal by seeking answers to fundamental science questions:

What is the inventory of solar system objects and what processes are active in and among them?

How did the Sun's family of planets, satellites, and minor bodies originate and evolve?

What are the characteristics of the solar system that lead to habitable environments?

How and where could life begin and evolve in the solar system?

What are characteristics of small bodies and planetary environments that pose hazards and/or provide resources?

Discovery Program

NASA's Discovery Program gives scientists the opportunity to dig deep into their imaginations and find innovative ways to unlock the mysteries of the solar system. It represents a breakthrough in the way NASA explores space, with lower-cost, highly focused planetary science investigations designed to enhance our understanding of the solar system.

Discovery Program Overview

NASA's Discovery Program gives scientists the opportunity to dig deep into their imaginations and find innovative ways to unlock the mysteries of the solar system. When it began in 1992, this program represented a breakthrough in the way NASA explores space. For the first time, scientists and engineers were called on to assemble teams and design exciting, focused planetary science investigations that would deepen the knowledge about our solar system.

As a complement to NASA's larger "flagship" planetary science explorations, the Discovery Program goal is to achieve outstanding results by launching many smaller missions using fewer resources and shorter development times. The main objective is to enhance our understanding of the solar system by exploring the planets, their moons, and small bodies such as comets and asteroids. The program also seeks to improve performance through the use of new technology and broaden university and industry participation in NASA missions

Discovery was among the first NASA programs to require a plan for education and public outreach, as NASA recognized the importance of communicating the excitement and meaning of space exploration to students and the public. Innovative methods that support national education initiatives are being developed to reach students of all ages.

All completed Discovery missions have achieved ground-breaking science, each taking a unique approach to space exploration, doing what's never been done before, and driving new technology innovations that may also improve life on Earth.

Earth Science Enterprise

Studying Earth from space provides a unique global perspective on our home planet's dynamic system of continents, oceans, atmosphere, ice and life. NASA's Earth Science missions seek to understand how Earth is changing and the consequences to life on Earth.

EARTH

New Report: Responding to the Challenge of Climate and Environmental Change

NASA's Plan for a Climate-Centric Architecture for Earth Observations and Applications from Space Earth is a complex, dynamic system we do not yet fully understand. The Earth system, like the human body, comprises diverse components that interact in complex ways. We need to understand the Earth's atmosphere, lithosphere, hydrosphere, cryosphere, and biosphere as a single connected system. Our planet is changing on all spatial and temporal scales. The purpose of NASA's Earth science program is to develop a scientific understanding of Earth's system and its response to natural or human-induced changes, and to improve prediction of climate, weather, and natural hazards.

NASA recently completed deployment of the Earth Observing System, the world's most advanced and comprehensive capability to measure global climate change. Over the coming decade, NASA and the Agency's research partners will be analyzing EOS data to characterize, understand, and predict variability and trends in Earth's system for both research and applications. Earth is the only planet we know to be capable of sustaining life. It is our lifeboat in the vast expanse of space. Over the past 50 years, world population has doubled, grain yields have tripled and economic output has grown sevenfold. Earth science research can ascertain whether and how the Earth can sustain this growth in the future. Also, over a third of the US economy – $3 trillion annually – is influenced by climate, weather, space weather, and natural hazards, providing economic incentive to study the Earth.

NASA Earth System Science conducts and sponsors research, collects new observations from space, develops technologies and extends science and technology education to learners of all ages. We work closely with our global partners in government, industry, and the public to enhance economic security, and environmental stewardship, benefiting society in many tangible ways. We conduct and sponsor research to answer fundamental science questions about the changes we see in climate, weather, and natural hazards, and deliver sound science that helps decision-makers make informed decisions. We inspire the next generation of explorers by providing opportunities for learners of all ages to investigate the Earth system using unique NASA resources, and our Earth System research is strengthening science, technology, engineering and mathematics education nationwide. This is a fundamental part of our mission because the leaders and citizens who will meet challenges of tomorrow are the students of today.

MISSIONS

In order to study the Earth as a whole system and understand how it is changing, NASA develops and supports a large number of Earth observing missions. These missions provide Earth science researchers the necessary data to address key questions about global climate change.

Missions begin with a study phase during which the key science objectives of the mission are identified, and designs for spacecraft and instruments are analyzed. Following a successful study phase, missions enter a development phase whereby all aspects of the mission are developed and tested to ensure that they meet the mission objectives. Operating missions are those missions that are currently active and providing science data to researchers. Operating missions may be in their primary operational phase or in an extended operational phase.

Senior Reviews for Earth Operating Missions:

- 2009 Senior Review

o   Science Panel Report

o   National Interest Sub-Panel Report

o   Technical & Cost Sub-Panel Report (TBS)

- 2007 Senior Review

o   2007 NASA Earth Science CoMRP Report

o   2007 NASA Earth Science Senior Review – Education/Public Outreach

o   2007 NASA Earth Science Senior Review Report

Exploration Systems Enterprise

Why Do We Explore?

From the time of our birth, humans have felt a primordial urge to explore — to blaze new trails, map new lands, and answer profound questions about ourselves and our universe.

The mission of NASA's Exploration Systems Enterprise is to conduct safe, sustained and affordable human and robotic exploration of Earth's Moon, Mars and beyond.

This new era in human exploration will leverage American ingenuity and propel the nation on a new journey of innovation and discovery. Groundbreaking new technologies will enable exploration of new worlds and increase our understanding of the Earth, our solar system and the universe beyond. Further collaborations on the International Space Station will increase NASA's return on investment and provide an optimal test bed for space technology research and development. In order to place NASA's focus on this forward-looking space enterprise, the President's Budget Request proposes cancelling the Constellation Program.

NASA doesn't intend to embark on this new journey alone. Commercial and international partnerships will benefit from a collective spirit of discovery and adventure, and will reduce the cost of space exploration by employing new business practices and leveraging common goals. NASA also invites citizen stakeholders to participate and share in the excitement of space exploration through upcoming initiatives designed to educate as well as glean new, creative ideas from standard and unconventional contributors.

We invite you to read below about the study teams that have been formed to develop strategies for the proposed new programs. Plans will continue to evolve with the next step of House and Senate appropriations.

NASA is pleased to release this summary of the agency's recent work on future human space exploration capabilities and missions, largely performed by our Human Exploration Framework Team (HEFT).

The agency established the HEFT last year to analyze exploration and technology concepts and provide inputs to the agency's senior leadership on the key components of a safe, sustainable, affordable and credible future human space exploration endeavor for the nation. The team's work helps provide a context for the next stage of NASA's diverse portfolio of activities and a basis for ongoing architecture analysis and program planning. HEFT's analysis focused on affordability, cost, performance, schedule, technology, and partnership considerations, while also identifying capabilities and destinations for future exploration as we move out, step by step, into the solar system.

HEFT has found that the most robust path for NASA in human space flight is a capability-driven approach where evolving capabilities would enable increasingly complex human exploration missions over time. A capability-driven framework also provides increased flexibility, greater cost effectiveness, and sustainability. Our strategy will open up many potential destinations for human spaceflight throughout the solar system, including the moon, near Earth asteroids, and Mars.

In NASA's framework, the four initial priorities are:

1) A human-rated Space Launch System, or heavy lift rocket;

2) A Multi-Purpose Crew Vehicle;

3) Commercial crew and cargo services to low Earth orbit, including the International Space Station; and

4) Mission-focused technologies to support expanded exploration capabilities in the future.

This summary provides information to facilitate discussions as the agency moves into the implementation phase of its new direction established in the NASA Authorization Act of 2010. Our intention is to provide effective assessment of the available information to support a roadmap that is affordable, sustainable and realistic. In line with future budget allocations and policy, we will continue to refine our strategic approach to short, mid and long term plans that will be leveraged by increasing capabilities and deepening partnerships with other nations. As we continue our analysis, NASA looks forward to working closely with the Congress and the public to build a space program that is forward thinking and also serves critical needs of the American people today.

Explorers Program

More than 70 spacecraft have been part of NASA's Explorer Program, including America's first artificial satellite – Explorer 1. The program's goal is to provide frequent space flight opportunities with a series of low to moderate cost missions developed in a relatively short time frame.

Mars Exploration Program

NASA's Mars Exploration Program sends robotic explorers to study the Red Planet roughly every two years. Current NASA Mars missions: Mars Global Surveyor, Mars 2001 Odyssey and the Mars Exploration Rovers (right), Spirit and Opportunity.

The Mars Exploration Program

Since our first close-up picture of Mars in 1965, spacecraft voyages to the Red Planet have revealed a world strangely familiar, yet different enough to challenge our perceptions of what makes a planet work. Every time we feel close to understanding Mars, new discoveries send us straight back to the drawing board to revise existing theories.

You'd think Mars would be easier to understand. Like Earth, Mars has polar ice caps and clouds in its atmosphere, seasonal weather patterns, volcanoes, canyons and other recognizable features. However, conditions on Mars vary wildly from what we know on our own planet.

Over the past three decades, spacecraft have shown us that Mars is rocky, cold, and sterile beneath its hazy, pink sky. We've discovered that today's Martian wasteland hints at a formerly volatile world where volcanoes once raged, meteors plowed deep craters, and flash floods rushed over the land. And Mars continues to throw out new enticements with each landing or orbital pass made by our spacecraft.

The Defining Question for Mars Exploration: Life on Mars?

Among our discoveries about Mars, one stands out above all others: the possible presence of liquid water on Mars, either in its ancient past or preserved in the subsurface today. Water is key because almost everywhere we find water on Earth, we find life. If Mars once had liquid water, or still does today, it's compelling to ask whether any microscopic life forms could have developed on its surface. Is there any evidence of life in the planet's past? If so, could any of these tiny living creatures still exist today? Imagine how exciting it would be to answer, "Yes!!"

Even if Mars is devoid of past or present life, however, there's still much excitement on the horizon. We ourselves might become the "life on Mars" should humans choose to travel there one day. Meanwhile, we still have a lot to learn about this amazing planet and its extreme environments.

Our Exploration Strategy: Follow the Water!

To discover the possibilities for life on Mars–past, present or our own in the future–the Mars Program has developed an exploration strategy known as "Follow the Water."

Following the water begins with an understanding of the current environment on Mars. We want to explore observed features like dry riverbeds, ice in the polar caps and rock types that only form when water is present. We want to look for hot springs, hydrothermal vents or subsurface water reserves. We want to understand if ancient Mars once held a vast ocean in the northern hemisphere as some scientists believe and how Mars may have transitioned from a more watery environment to the dry and dusty climate it has today. Searching for these answers means delving into the planet's geologic and climate history to find out how, when and why Mars underwent dramatic changes to become the forbidding, yet promising, planet we observe today.

Future Missions

To pursue these goals, all of our future missions will be driven by rigorous scientific questions that will continuously evolve as we make new discoveries.

Brand new technologies will enable us to explore Mars in ways we never have before, resulting in higher-resolution images, precision landings, longer-ranging surface mobility and even the return of Martian soil and rock samples for studies in laboratories here on Earth.

Human Space Flight

NASA's Human Space Flight team has systematically developed the capability to live and work in space. Thousands of people work to keep astronauts living, working and researching in space aboard the International Space Station and Space Shuttle.

New Frontiers

Missions in NASA's New Frontiers Program will tackle specific solar system exploration goals identified in the Decadal Solar System Exploration Survey conducted by the Space Studies Board of the National Research Council. Proposed targets include Pluto and the Kuiper Belt, Jupiter, Venus, and sample returns from the surface of a comet and Earth's Moon. The program is designed enable high-quality planetary missions that require resources beyond those available in the lower-cost Discovery Program. The flight rate is expected to be about one mission every three years. The first New Frontiers mission is New Horizons.

New Millennium Program

The New Millennium Program tests breakthrough technologies in space before they become standard equipment on next-generation spacecraft. New Millennium solar system missions: Deep Space 1 and Deep Space 2.

NASA space science missions have ventured to the moon, explored other planets, traveled to the edges of our solar system, and peered back in time. They have also done what is sometimes even more difficult——studied our own planet, Earth.

These missions have provided astounding views of the universe and new knowledge of our solar system, but there is still so much more to "see" and learn. And, as missions become progressively more daring, and thus more difficult, more advanced capabilities are needed. However, before new, untried technologies are used for the first time on complex exploration missions, engineers and scientists want to make sure they will operate well, and safely, in the hazardous environment of space.

To accomplish this, NASA's Office of Space Science (OSS) and Office of Earth Science jointly established the New Millennium Program (NMP) in 1995——an ambitious, exciting vision to speed up space exploration through the development and testing of leading-edge technologies. A unique program, managed by the Jet Propulsion Laboratory/California Institute of Technology, NMP provides a critical bridge from initial concept to exploration-mission use. Through NMP, selected technologies are demonstrated in the "laboratory" of space that can't be replicated on Earth.

Since its inception over a decade ago, NMP has validated many innovative technologies for both Earth science and space science missions. Now funded and managed solely out of NASA's newly formed Science Mission Directorate (SMD), the Program continues to demonstrate advanced technologies that will enable space science missions of the 21st century with significant (a several-generation leap) technical capabilities.

Highly advanced technologies are key to more capable, powerful, and efficient spacecraft and science instruments. They are also key to gathering new and exciting scientific knowledge of our solar system and of our universe.

Origins Program

NASA's Origins Program seeks to answer questions that have endured since humans looked into the night sky: "Where did we come from?" and "Are we alone?" Origins scientists are from a wide range of scientific disciplines from astronomy, physics, and chemistry, to geology and paleontology, as well as micro- and evolutionary biology.

Project Prometheus

Project Prometheus was established in 2003 to develop technology in the areas of radioisotope power system and nuclear power and propulsion for exploration of the solar system. The project will develop the first reactor powered spacecraft and demonstrate that it can be operated safely and reliably on long duration space missions. The proposed Jupiter Icy Moons Orbiter will be the first space science mission to use the new technology.

Sounding Rockets

Wallops manages NASA's Sounding Rocket Program and is responsible for all aspects of a mission, from the launch vehicle, to payload design and development and data retrieval. Scientific data are collected and returned to Earth by telemetry links, which transfer the data from the sounding rocket payload to the researchers on the ground. In most cases, the payload parachutes back to Earth, where it is recovered and reused.

Scientific Balloons

Balloons have been used for decades to conduct scientific studies. While the basics of ballooning have not changed, balloon size has increased and their dependability has improved greatly. The Wallops Flight Facility manages the NASA Balloon Program, which offers capabilities and benefits for scientific research that cannot be duplicated by other methods.

Structure and Evolution of the Universe

The Structure and Evolution of the Universe program seeks to explore and understand the dynamic transformations of energy in the Universe—the entire web of biological and physical interactions that determine the evolution of our cosmic habitat. This search for understanding will enrich the human spirit and inspire a new generation of explorers, scientists, and engineers.

Overview

The Astrophysics Science Division conducts a broad program of research in astronomy, astrophysics, and fundamental physics. Individual investigations address issues such as the nature of dark matter and dark energy, which planets outside our solar system may harbor life, and the nature of space, time, and matter at the edges of black holes.

Observing photons, particles, and gravitational waves enables researchers to probe astrophysical objects and processes. Researchers develop theoretical models, design experiments and hardware to test theories, interpret and evaluate the data, archive and disseminate the data, provide expert user support to the scientific community, and publish conclusions drawn from research. The Division also conducts education and public outreach programs about its projects and missions.

Sun-Earth Connection

The SEC Division investigates the physics of the Sun, the heliosphere, the local interstellar medium, and all planetary environments within the heliosphere. Taken together, these studies encompass the scientific disciplines of solar physics, heliospheric physics, magnetospheric physics, and aeronomy. They address problems such as solar variability, the responses of the planets to such variability, and the interaction of the heliosphere with the galaxy.

Near Earth Objects (NEO)—

History of Comets–

Comets are the remainders of material formed in the coldest part of our solar system. Impacts from comets played a major role in the evolution of the Earth, primarily during its early history billions of years ago. Some believe that they brought water and a variety of organic molecules to Earth. Take a look at what Ancient Cultures thought of comets.

Comets are visible for two reasons. Dust driven from a comet's nucleus reflects sunlight as it travels through space. Secondly, certain gases, stimulated by the sun, give off light like fluorescent light bulbs. Over time a comet may become less active or even dormant.

Scientists are anxious to learn whether comets exhaust their supply of gas and ice to space or seal it into their interiors. What is the difference between the interior of a comet's nucleus and its surface? Controlled cratering like that planned for Deep Impact allows a look deep into the interior of the comet. Investigators anticipate that a look inside comet Tempel 1 will unlock the treasures a comet has to offer.

Comet Tempel 1 was discovered in 1867. Although few physical data are available, it appears to be a comet with relatively little surface activity. Orbiting the sun every 5.5 years, it has probably made more than one hundred passages through the inner solar system. This makes it a good target to study evolutionary change in the mantle or upper crust of the comet.

Studies of brightness variations with time indicate that the comet rotates much more slowly than Earth. Its rotation will not take the impact crater out of the spacecraft's field of view during the encounter period.

Comets in Ancient Cultures-Comets have inspired dread, fear, and awe in many different cultures and societies around the world and throughout time. They have been branded with such titles as "the Harbinger of Doom" and "the Menace of the Universe."

They have been regarded both as omens of disaster and messengers of the gods. Why is it that comets are some of the most feared and venerated objects in the night sky? Why did so many cultures cringe at the sight of a comet?

When people living in ancient cultures looked up, comets were the most remarkable objects in the night sky. Comets were unlike any other object in the night sky. Whereas most celestial bodies travel across the skies at regular, predictable intervals, so regular that constellations could be mapped and predicted, comets' movements have always seemed very erratic and unpredictable. This led people in many cultures to believe that the gods dictated their motions and were sending them as a message.

What were the gods trying to say? Some cultures read the message by the images that they saw upon looking at the comet. For example, to some cultures the tail of the comet gave it the appearance of the head of a woman, with long flowing hair behind her. This sorrowful symbol of mourning was understood to mean the gods that had sent the comet to earth were displeased.

Others thought that the elongated comet looked like a fiery sword blazing across the night sky, a traditional sign of war and death. Such a message from the gods could only mean that their wrath would soon be unleashed onto the people of the land. Such ideas struck fear into those who saw comets dart across the sky. The likeness of the comet, though, was not the only thing that inspired fear.

Ancient cultural legends also played a hand in inspiring a terrible dread of these celestial nomads. The Roman prophecies, the "Sibylline Oracles," spoke of a "great conflagration from the sky, falling to earth," while the most ancient known mythology, the Babylonian "Epic of Gilgamesh," described fire, brimstone, and flood with the arrival of a comet.

Rabbi Moses Ben Nachman, a Jew living in Spain, wrote of God taking two stars from Khima and throwing them at the Eearth in order to begin the great flood. Yakut legend in ancient Mongolia called comets "the daughter of the devil," and warned of destruction, storm and frost, whenever she approaches the earth. Stories associating comets with such terrible imagery are at the base of so many cultures on Earth, and fuel a dread that followed comet sightings throughout history.

Comets' influence on cultures is not limited simply to tales of myth and legend, though. Comets throughout history have been blamed for some of history's darkest times. In Switzerland, Halley's Comet was blamed for earthquakes, illnesses, red rain, and even the births of two-headed animals.

The Romans recorded that a fiery comet marked the assassination of Julius Caesar, and another was blamed for the extreme bloodshed during the battle between Pompey and Caesar. In

England, Halley's Comet was blamed for bringing the Black Death. The Incas, in South America, even record a comet having foreshadowed Francisco Pizarro's arrival just days before he brutally conquered them.

Comets and disaster became so intertwined that Pope Calixtus III even excommunicated Halley's Comet as an instrument of the devil, and a meteorite, from a comet, became enshrined as one of the most venerated objects in all of Islam. Were it not for a Chinese affinity for meticulous record keeping, a true understanding of comets may never have been reached.

Unlike their Western counterparts, Chinese astronomers kept extensive records on the appearances, paths, and disappearances of hundreds of comets. Extensive comet atlases have been found dating back to the Han Dynasty, which describe comets as "long-tailed pheasant stars" or "broom stars" and associate the different cometary forms with different disasters.

Although the Chinese also regarded comets as "vile stars," their extensive records allowed later astronomers to determine the true nature of comets.

Although most human beings no longer cringe at the sight of a comet, they still inspire fear everywhere around the globe, from Hollywood to doomsday cults. The United States even set up the Near Earth Asteroid Tracking (NEAT) program specifically to guard us from these "divine" dangers." However, although they were once regarded as omens of disaster, and messengers of the god(s), today a scientific approach has helped allay such concerns.

It is science and reason that has led the fight against this fear since the days of the ancients. It is science and reason that has emboldened the human spirit enough to venture out and journey to a comet. It is science and reason that will unlock the secrets that they hold.

Deep Impact Mission–

What is deep inside a comet?

Comets are time capsules that hold clues about the formation and evolution of the solar system. They are composed of ice, gas and dust, primitive debris from the solar system's distant and coldest regions that formed 4.5 billion years ago. Deep Impact, a NASA Discovery Mission, is the first space mission to probe beneath the surface of a comet and reveal the secrets of its interior.

On July 4, 2005, the Deep Impact spacecraft arrives at Comet Tempel 1 to impact it with a 370-kg (~820-lbs) mass. On impact, the crater produced is expected to range in size from that of a house to that of a football stadium, and two to fourteen stories deep. Ice and dust debris is ejected from the crater revealing fresh material beneath. Sunlight reflecting off the ejected material provides a dramatic brightening that fades slowly as the debris dissipates into space or falls back onto the comet. Images from cameras and a spectrometer are sent to Earth covering the approach, the impact and its aftermath. The effects of the collision with the comet will also be observable from certain locations on Earth and in some cases with smaller telescopes. The data is analyzed and combined with that of other NASA and international comet missions. Results from these missions will lead to a better understanding of both the solar system's formation and implications of comets colliding with Earth.

The Mission

The Deep Impact mission lasts six years from start to finish. Planning and design for the mission took place from November 1999 through May 2001. The mission team is proceeding with the building and testing of the two-part spacecraft. The larger "flyby" spacecraft carries a smaller "impactor" spacecraft to Tempel 1 and releases it into the comet's path for a planned collision.

In December 2004, a Delta II rocket launches the combined Deep Impact spacecraft which leaves Earth's orbit and is directed toward the comet. The combined spacecraft approaches Tempel 1 and collects images of the comet before the impact. In early July 2005, 24 hours before impact, the flyby spacecraft points high-precision tracking telescopes at the comet and releases the impactor on a course to hit the comet's sunlit side.

The impactor is a battery-powered spacecraft that operates independently of the flyby spacecraft for just one day. It is called a "smart" impactor because, after its release, it takes over its own navigation and manoeuvres into the path of the comet. A camera on the impactor captures and relays images of the comet's nucleus just seconds before collision. The impact is not forceful enough to make an appreciable change in the comet's orbital path around the Sun.

After release of the impactor, the flyby spacecraft manoeuvres to a new path that, at closest approach passes 500 km (300 miles) from the comet. The flyby spacecraft observes and records the impact, the ejected material blasted from the crater, and the structure and composition of the crater's interior. After its shields protect it from the comet's dust tail passing overhead, the flyby spacecraft turns to look at the comet again. The flyby spacecraft takes additional data from the other side of the nucleus and observes changes in the comet's activity. While the flyby spacecraft and impactor do their jobs, professional and amateur astronomers at both large and small telescopes on Earth observe the impact and its aftermath, and results are broadcast over the Internet.

Comet Tempel 1

Comet Tempel 1 was discovered in 1867 by Ernst Tempel. The comet has made many passages through the inner solar system orbiting the Sun every 5.5 years. This makes Tempel 1 a good target to study evolutionary change in the mantle, or upper crust. Comets are visible for two reasons. First, dust driven from a comet's nucleus reflects sunlight as it travels through space. Second, certain gases in the comet's coma, stimulated by the Sun, give off light like a fluorescent bulb. Over time, a comet may become less active or even dormant. Scientists are eager to learn whether comets exhaust their supply of gas and dust to space or seal it into their interiors. They would also like to learn about the structure of a comet's interior and how it is different from its surface. The controlled cratering experiment of this mission provides answers to these questions.

Technical Implementation

The flyby spacecraft carries a set of instruments and the smart impactor. Two instruments on the flyby spacecraft observe the impact, crater and debris with optical imaging and infrared spectral mapping. The flyby spacecraft uses an X-band radio antenna (transmission at about eight gigahertz) to communicate to Earth as it also listens to the impactor on a different frequency. For most of the mission, the flyby spacecraft communicates through the 34-meter antennae of NASA's Deep Space Network. During the short period of encounter and impact, when there is an increase in volume of data, overlapping antennas around the world are used. Primary data is transmitted immediately and other data is transmitted over the following week. The impactor spacecraft is composed mainly of copper, which is not expected to appear in data from a comet's composition. For its short period of operation, the impactor uses simpler versions of the flyby spacecraft's hardware and software – and fewer backup systems.

The Team

The Deep Impact mission is a partnership among the University of Maryland (UMD), the California Institute of Technology's Jet Propulsion Laboratory (JPL) and Ball Aerospace and Technology Corp. The scientific leadership of the mission is based at UMD. Engineers at Ball Aerospace and Technologies Corp. design and build the spacecraft under JPL's management. Engineers at JPL control the spacecraft after launch and relay data to scientists for analysis. The entire team consists of more than 250 scientists, engineers, managers, and educators. Deep Impact is a NASA Discovery Mission, eighth in a series of low-cost, highly focused space science investigations. Deep Impact offers an extensive outreach program in partnership with other comet and asteroid missions and institutions to benefit the public, educational and scientific communities.

The Comet-Tempel-1

Discovery

Comet 9P/Tempel 1 was discovered on April 3, 1867 by Ernst Wilhelm Leberecht Tempel of Marseilles France while visually searching for comets. The comet was then 9th magnitude and described by Tempel as having an apparent diameter of 4 to 5 arcmin across. Later calculations revealed that the comet had been situated 0.71 AU from the Earth and 1.64 AU from the sun at that time.

Historical Highlights

The comet was very well placed for its 1867 discovery thanks to its closest approach to Earth (0.568 AU) and its perihelion (1.562 AU), which occurred on May 15 and May 24, respectively. Over the next five months after its initial detection, subsequent observations were frequently made. The comet was last detected on August 27, 1867 by Julius Schmidt, at which point the comet had become too faint for position measurements. At that time the comet was 1.30 AU from Earth and 1.81 AU from the sun.

The comet was first recognized as periodic in May of 1867 when C. Bruhns of Leipzig determined the orbital period to be 5.74 years. By the time the final observations had been made of the 1867 apparition, the orbital period had been re-calculated to be 5.68 years.

The comet was recovered on April 4, 1873 by E.J.M. Stephan of Marseilles, France. The comet remained under observation until July 1st of that year.

Predictions were made for an 1879 return, with the most ambitious being that of Raoul Gautier who computed definitive orbits from the two previous appearances before making his predictions for the upcoming return. Gautier's predictions enabled Tempel to recover the comet on April 25, 1879. The comet was observed until its last detection on July 8.

In 1881, comet Tempel 1 passed 0.55 AU from Jupiter. Due to gravitational interactions, the comet's orbital period was increased to 6.5 years and the perihelion distance was increased from 1.8 AU to 2.1 AU, making the comet an even fainter object. Subsequently, the comet was lost and it was not observed at its next expected return. Photographic attempts during 1898 and 1905 failed to recover the comet.

During 1963, B.G. Marsden conducted an investigation as to why comet Tempel 1 became lost. He found that further close approaches to Jupiter in 1941 (0.41 AU) and 1953 (0.77 AU) had decreased both the perihelion distance and the orbital period to values smaller than when the comet was initially discovered. These approaches moved Tempel 1 into its present libration around the 1:2 resonance with Jupiter. Subsequently, Marsden published predictions for the 1967 and 1972 returns in his paper On the Orbits of Some Long Lost Comets. (Courtesy of NASA Astrophysics Data System)

Despite an unfavorable 1967 return, Elizabeth Roemer of the Catalina Observatory took several photographs during 1967. Her initial inspections of these photographs revealed nothing. However, in late 1968 she re-examined the photographic plates and found that a single exposure taken on June 8, 1967 held the image of an 18th magnitude diffuse object very close to where Marsden had predicted the comet to be. Unfortunately, the single image did not provide definitive proof of the comet's recovery.

During 1972, Marsden's predictions allowed Roemer and L.M. Vaughn to recover the comet on January 11 from Steward Observatory. The comet became widely observed and reached a maximum brightness of magnitude 11 during May of that year. The comet was last seen on July 10. This apparition proved that the single image taken by Roemer in 1967 was indeed comet 9P/Tempel 1. Since that time the comet has been seen at every apparition.

Tempel 1 Before Its Discovery

Long term integrations of comet 9P/Tempel 1's orbit suggest that the perihelion distance has been inside 10 AU for at least 3×105 years. The aphelion distance is much less well determined far in the past. The inclination of Tempel 1's orbit has remained low for as far into the past as the integrations have been calculated.

Spacecraft and Instruments–

The Deep Impact Spacecraft

The flight system consists of two spacecraft: the flyby spacecraft and the impactor. Each spacecraft has its own instruments and capabilities to receive and transmit data.

The flyby spacecraft carries the primary imaging instruments (the HRI and MRI) and the impactor (with an ITS) to the vicinity of the comet nucleus.

It releases the impactor, receives impactor data, supports the instruments as they image the impact and resulting crater, and then transmits the science data back to Earth.

Image at Right: This illustration shows the Deep Impact two-part vehicle consisting of a flyby spacecraft and the impactor. Image credit: NASA

The impactor guides itself to hit the comet nucleus on the sunlit side. The energy from the impact will excavate a crater approximately 100m wide and 28m deep.

The instruments help guide both spacecrafts and then acquire the science data that will be analyzed by the science team.

The Boeing Delta II Launch Vehicle

Before the flight system can get to the comet, it has to be delivered into space.

The Deep Impact mission will be launched aboard a Boeing Delta II 2925 rocket with the dual spacecraft tucked within the Delta's fairing.

The Delta II launch vehicles are descended from the Delta rockets that have been in use since the 1960s. They have carried aloft a number of NASA spacecraft like Deep Space 1, NEAR, Mars Climate Orbiter, Mars Polar Lander, STARDUST, FUSE, IMAGE and EO-1/SAC-C into space.

3.4.19-Feature of Spacecraft-

Technology – Flight System

11.19.04

The flight system consists of two spacecraft: the flyby spacecraft and the impactor. Each spacecraft has its own instruments and capabilities to receive and transmit data.

The flyby spacecraft carries the primary imaging instruments (the HRI and MRI) and the impactor (with an ITS) to the vicinity of the comet nucleus. It releases the impactor, receives impactor data, supports the instruments as they image the impact and resulting crater, and then transmits the science data back to Earth.

The impactor guides itself to hit the comet nucleus on the sunlit side. The energy from the impact will excavate a crater approximately 100m wide and 28m deep.

The instruments help guide both spacecrafts and then acquire the science data that will be analyzed by the science team.

Main Goals of the Flight System:

- Hit nucleus of Tempel 1 with sufficient kinetic energy to form a crater with a depth > 20m
- Observe nucleus for > 10 minutes following impact
- Image nucleus impact, crater development and inside of crater
- Obtain spectrometry of nucleus and inside of crater
- Acquire, store, format, and downlink imagery and spectrometry data

Feature of Flyby Spacecraft

11.23.04

As part of Deep Impact's Flight System, the flyby spacecraft is one of two vessels carrying the three science Instruments. Ball Aerospace & Technologies Corp. designed the spacecraft specifically for the Deep Impact mission.

The flyby spacecraft features a high throughput RAD750 CPU with 1553 data bus-based avionics architecture, and a high stability pointing control system. Spacecraft optical navigation and conventional ground-based navigation will facilitate maneuvering the flyby spacecraft as close as possible to the collision course with comet Tempel 1. When the impactor is released from its union with the flyby spacecraft, the flyby spacecraft will slow itself down and align itself to observe the impact, ejecta, crater development, and crater interior as it passes within 500 km of Tempel 1. It will also receive data from the impactor and transfer it to the Deep Space Network ground receivers.

The flyby spacecraft carries two of the three primary instruments, the High Resolution Instrument (HRI) and the Medium Resolution Instrument (MRI), for imaging, infrared spectroscopy, and optical navigation.

About the size of a Ford Explorer, the flyby spacecraft is three-axis stabilized and uses a fixed solar array and a small NiH2 battery for its power system. The structure is aluminium and aluminium honeycomb construction. Blankets, surface radiators, finishes, and heaters passively control the temperature. The propulsion system employs a simple blowdown hydrazine design that provides 190 m/s of delta V. The flyby spacecraft mass is 650 kg.

During the encounter phase, a high gain antenna transmits near-real-time images of the impact back to Earth. The flyby spacecraft uses X-band to communicate to Earth and S-band to communicate with the impactor after separation.

Debris shielding is a key part of the flyby S/C design. As the spacecraft passes through the inner coma of the comet it is in danger of being hit by small particles that could damage the control, imaging and communication systems. To minimize this potential damage the spacecraft is rotated before it passes through the inner coma allowing debris shielding to provide complete protection to the flyby spacecraft and instrument elements.

Payload Power: 92 W average during engagement

Payload Mass: 370 kg impactor, 90 kg instruments

Payload Total Data Volume: 309 Mbytes

Payload Data Downlinked: 309 Mbytes

Pointing Accuracy: 200 microradian

(inst. boresight orientation)

Pointing Knowledge: 65 microradian 3 axes 3-sigma

Telecom Band to Earth: X-band

Uplink/Downlink Rates: 125 bps/175 Kbps

(exclusive of Reed-Solomon encoding)

Telecom Band to Impactor: S-band

Data Rate to Impactor: 64 Kbps @ max range (8,700 km)

Propulsion/RCS: 190 m/s divert;

5000 N-s RCS total impulse

Deep Impact's Impactor

The impactor separates from the flyby spacecraft 24 hours before it impacts the surface of Tempel 1's nucleus. The impactor delivers 19 Gigajoules (that's 4.8 tons of TNT) of kinetic energy to excavate the crater. This kinetic energy is generated by the combination of the mass of the impactor (370 kg; 816 lbs) and its velocity when it impacts (~10.2 km/s). Targeting and hitting the comet in a lit area is one of the mission's greatest challenges since the impactor will be traveling at 10 km per second and it must hit an area less than 6 km (3.7 miles) in diameter from about 864,000 km (536,865 miles) away. To accomplish this feat, the impactor uses a high-precision star tracker, the Impactor Target Sensor (ITS), and Auto-Navigation algorithms (developed by Jet Propulsion Laboratory for the DS-1 mission) to guide it to the target. Minor trajectory corrections and attitude control are available by using the impactor's small hydrazine propulsion system.

The impactor is made primarily of copper (49%) as opposed to aluminium (24%) because it minimizes corruption of spectral emission lines that are used to analyze the nucleus.The impactor is mechanically and electrically attached to the flyby spacecraft for all but the last 24 hours of the mission. Only during the last 24 hours does the impactor run on internal battery power. The propulsion system uses hydrazine that can provide 25 m/s of delta-V for targeting.

System Requirement Specifications for the Impactor

Image Data Volume: Approximately 17 Mbytes (about 35 images) total

Pointing Accuracy: 2 mrad 3-sigma (targeting sensor boresight orientation)

Pointing Knowledge: 150 microradian 3 axes 3-sigma

Targeting Accuracy: 300 m 3-sigma WRT nucleus center of brightness

Telecom Band: S-Band

Data Rate to S/C: 64 Kbps @ max range (8,700 km)

Command Rate: 16 Kbps

Energy Storage: 2.8 Kw-hr for baseline 24 hr mission

Propulsion/RCS: 25 m/s divert; 1750 N-s RCS impulse

3.4.24-Technology – Instruments

Built by Ball Aerospace & Technologies Corp., the Deep Impact instruments have two purposes. They guide the flyby spacecraft and impactor onto a collision course with the comet and they take the science data before, during, and after the impact. The instruments are designed so that they satisfy the following science requirements:

Pre-impact Imaging Requirements:

Observe the comet and targeted impact site prior to impact, acquiring spatial and spectral data

Ejecta Imaging Requirements:

Observe the ejecta and track the movement of the ejecta curtain from crater to coma

Crater Evolution Data Requirements:

Observe the crater and surface evolution

Pristine Crater Data Requirements: Observe the exposed pristine crater surface features via spectral imagers with increasing resolution

Modular Design Requirements:

Have opto-mechanically interchangeable focal plane modules

The primary instruments on the flyby spacecraft are the High Resolution Instrument (HRI) and the Medium Resolution Instrument (MRI). The HRI, one of the largest space-based instruments built specifically for planetary science, is the main science camera for Deep Impact. It provides the highest resolution images via a combined visible camera, an infrared spectrometer, and a special imaging module. The HRI is optimally suited to observe the comet's nucleus. The MRI serves as the functional backup for the HRI, and is slightly better at navigation for the last 10 days of travel before impact due its wider field of view, which allows it to observe more stars around the comet. The difference between the two is the telescope, which sets the field of view (FOV) and the resolution of each. .

The ITS on the impactor is nearly identical to the MRI as it uses the same type of telescope as the MRI as well as the same type of CCD that is in the MRI's Multi Spectral CCD Camera but differs only in that it lacks the filter wheel.

Technology – Instruments

Built by Ball Aerospace & Technologies Corp., the Deep Impact instruments have two purposes. They guide the flyby spacecraft and impactor onto a collision course with the comet and they take the science data before, during, and after the impact. The instruments are designed so that they satisfy the following science requirements:

Pre-impact Imaging Requirements:

Observe the comet and targeted impact site prior to impact, acquiring spatial and spectral data

Ejecta Imaging Requirements:

Observe the ejecta and track the movement of the ejecta curtain from crater to coma

Crater Evolution Data Requirements:

Observe the crater and surface evolution

Pristine Crater Data Requirements:

Observe the exposed pristine crater surface features via spectral imagers with increasing resolution

Modular Design Requirements:

Have opto-mechanically interchangeable focal plane modules

The primary instruments on the flyby spacecraft are the High Resolution Instrument (HRI) and the Medium Resolution Instrument (MRI). The HRI, one of the largest space-based instruments built specifically for planetary science, is the main science camera for Deep Impact. It provides the highest resolution images via a combined visible camera, an infrared spectrometer, and a special imaging module. The HRI is optimally suited to observe the comet's nucleus. The MRI serves as the functional backup for the HRI, and is slightly better at navigation for the last 10 days of travel before impact due its wider field of view, which allows it to observe more stars around the comet. The difference between the two is the telescope, which sets the field of view (FOV) and the resolution of each.

The ITS on the impactor is nearly identical to the MRI as it uses the same type of telescope as the MRI as well as the same type of CCD that is in the MRI's Multi Spectral CCD Camera but differs only in that it lacks the filter wheel.

In the span of one year I stayed with Professor Pandey, I became a close associate of his and a close confide and intact friend of him. Each day in the evening we would sit together at his residence and he would tell me the finer points of Archaeology and History, about problems in Ayodhya and Faizabad, about his meeting with a Cambridge University professor – Prof Dilip Chakraborty and about people in the University. I would listen to him very carefully while sipping a cup of tea.

I remember how closely he was associated with the concerns of the people in Ayodhya that when five terrorists beamed penetrated in to the disputed site. He immediately called a senior officer in the Home Ministry and narrated the whole incident and the problems. I would fight with him, debated with him but the next moment we would become good friends. He also gave me a task to translate one of his books which he wrote during the visit of his friend and Professor of Cambridge University – Professor Dilp Chakraborty. I started it and completed within a span of one month for which he appreciated me and gave me the e-mail address of Professor Dilip Chakraborty.

In a way he mentored me for a span of one year until my new job with another University in February 2006. For fone year between February 2005 and -February 2006, we shared many secrets and many stories. He died in 2010, when he met with a minor accident and was shifted to a Delhi hospital. It was purely a shock for me when I heard about professor's untimely death, about which I have narrated in 'Dispatch-13' in "The Nose of the News" segment.

Terror Attacks in Ayodhya

Apart from lecturing in the University, I changed my routine in daily life. I tried to leave all my worries and the people of Delhi and Bangalore aside. My routine was to get up early in the morning and then to take my bicycle out and go to a gym close to my village. The gym was located near a mosque and many Muslim boys were regulars at that gym. It gave me a healthy feeling. By 10:00 am I would again ride my bicycle and go to the University for lectures. By evening I would be tired and after taking an early dinner every night would go to sleep.

It was on the morning of 5th July and when I was gymming, a group of Muslim boys came running inside and shouted, "Are Un Logon ne Attack Kar Diya Hai,"(Oh, those people have attacked). Before I could understand anything and came out of the gym, news spread like a fire. I returned to my village, and then I got to know the truth. One of my cousin brothers told me that some terrorists had entered the disputed site and a fierce gun battle was going on with security forces.

I again took my bicycle out and reached my uncle's house in Ayodhya. Midway I heard people talking about a terrorist attack behind closed doors. It was the first of its kind in Ayodhya. Terrorists had tried to enter a certain temple before as well, but this time it was a neck-to-neck fight. As I reached my uncle's house I saw the entire area was cordoned off and each street of Ayodhya had been occupied by security forces.

The gun battle was still going on and there was a rumor that the terrorists were staying in Ayodhya for the past seven days in the get-up of 'Pandas' (priests). They confided in another 'panda' who helped them to allow him to visit the site. However, he did it without knowing their intentions.

My uncle's only son, who was the eldest among all of us, took me to the site where the battle had already finished. All the terrorists were gunned down. There were five. While security forces and police kept searching nearby areas suspecting if any one of them would have hidden, the media gathered at the disputed site.

All five terrorists succeeded in ramming into the disputed site by blowing off the security barricade, and while they intended to attack 'Garb Griha' (Sanctum Sanctorum), they came under fire by security forces deployed heavily in and around the disputed site. Security forces cleared the area and gave a 'Press Conference' before the media people. The security vigilance was kept on high alert for the next week and many suspects were arrested from nearby areas.

I filed two reports in the coming months about this incident, again to more than two dozen individuals and organizations.

Thread-1:

Six heavily armed terrorists, who made an attempt to storm the high-security makeshift Ram temple in Ayodhya, were killed before they could make it to the shrine.

The attackers came in an ambassador car at around 0900 IST, following an explosive-laden jeep, which they rammed into the security barricade to breach the cordon.

While one militant who rammed the jeep was blown to pieces, five others were killed in the encounter with security personnel, Faizabad Commissioner Arun Sinha said.

Sources said that a woman devotee, who happened to be near the scene of blast, also succumbed to her injuries in the hospital, official sources here said.

Police sources said that the militants were disguised as devotees.

The barricade and the protective wall collapsed as a result of the explosion and the militants were able to gain entry into the campus through the Sita rasoi (kitchen), Sinha said.

He said the security personnel however intercepted them.

Police sources said that the arrested driver Rehan is a resident of Ayodhya, and he was being interrogated.

Four AK 47 and AK 56 rifles, some hand grenades and ammunition were recovered from the bodies of the slain militants, they said.

This is the first terrorist attack on the disputed complex since the makeshift temple came up after the demolition of the Babri mosque 13 years ago.

Thread-2:

On 5 July 2005, five terrorists attacked the makeshift Ram temple at the site of the destroyed Babri Mosque in Ayodhya, India. All five were shot dead in the ensuing gunfight with the Central Reserve Police Force (CRPF), while one civilian died in the grenade attack that the terrorists launched in order to breach the cordoned wall. The CRPF suffered three casualties, two of whom were seriously injured with multiple gunshot wounds.

On 5 July 2005, the heavily guarded Shri Ram Janambhoomi-Babri Masjid complex, the site of the destroyed Mosque and, according to Hindus, the birthplace of God Shri Ram, at Ayodhya in Uttar Pradesh state of India was attacked by heavily-armed terrorists. The attack was foiled by security officials and the attackers were killed.

The terrorists are believed to be from the terrorist organization Lashkar-e-Toiba, and are believed to have entered India through Nepal. They posed as pilgrims to Ayodhya and boarded a Tata Sumo at Akbarpur near the Kichaucha village in Faizabad. At Faizabad they abandoned the Sumo and hired a jeep driven by a driver, Rehan Alam Amsari. According to a statement by the driver, the terrorists visited the Shri Ram Mandir (Temple) at Ayodhya where they prayed, possibly to reinforce the impression that they were indeed pilgrims. The terrorists then drove the jeep into the Shri Ram Janambhoomi and forced the driver out of the vehicle, banging the jeep against the security cordon. At 9:05 am, they hurled M67 hand grenades from 50 metres away to breach the cordon fence. Ramesh Pandey, a pilgrim guide who happened to be near the site at this moment, 50 m away from the terrorists, died on the spot as a result of the grenade blast. Firing indiscriminately, the 5 terrorists entered Mata Sita Rasoi. Returning the gunfire, a platoon of 35 CRPF soldiers killed all five of the fighters in a gunfight that lasted for over an hour. Three CRPF soldiers also received serious injuries and, as of July 2008, two remain comatose. All the terrorists died within 100 meters of the site.

It is suspected that the terrorists belonged to the group Lashkar-e-Toiba. The investigating team is tracking the phone calls made from the cell phones using the IMEI numbers. The pPolice recovered a single RPG-7 rocket-propelled grenade launcher, five Type 56 assault rifles, five M1911 pistols, several M67 grenades and some jihadi documents.

Rehan Alam, the jeep driver, was detained by the police for further investigations.

On 28 July 2005, four men from Jammu and Kashmir– Akbar Hussain, Lal Mohammad, Mohmmad Naseer and Mohmmad Rafeeq– were arrested in connection with the attack. On 3 August 2005, another four men– Asif Iqbal, Mohd Aziz, Mohd Nasim and Shaqeel Ahmed– were arrested on suspicion of involvement in the bombing. A fifth man, Irfan Khan, was arrested a few days earlier.

Most of India's political organizations condemned the attack as barbaric and requested people to maintain law and order. The Rashtriya Swayamsevak Sangh, its offshoot the Vishva Hindu Parishad and the Bharatiya Janata Party (BJP) declared an India-wide protest and bandh on 8 July 2005. BJP president L.K. Advani called for reinstatement of the Prevention of Terrorist Activities Act (POTA) in the wake of the attack.

Contract Lectureship and My Marriage

Lectures on Space Exploration in the University, discussions with Professor Pandey on the minutest parts of Archaeology and History, and dispatches to two dozen individuals as part of "The Nose of The News" were somehow satisfying my journalistic and creative instincts, but they were heavy on my pocket. Since I seldom got any payment from the University, I had to worry about finances which I had to put out to carry the episodes. One day, one of my neighbors in the village told me about a vacancy in another University in a nearby district, Jaunpur.

The vacancy was for the post of contract lectureship in the department of Journalism and Mass Communication, for three years. I checked the University website and it read-

Purvanchal University, Jaunpur renamed as Veer Bahadur Singh Purvanchal University in the honor of late Shri Veer Bahadur Singh, former Chief Minister of the state, was established on 2nd October 1987 as an affiliating university under U.P. State university University Act 1973. Continuous qualitative and quantitative growth, excellence in academic and administrative activities, transparent and efficient academic administration have been some of the distinct characteristics on the basis of which the university emerged as one of the leading universities of the state. Started with the 68 affiliated colleges, the university now has widened its spectrum of activities with 367 affiliated graduate and post-graduate colleges and students enrolment of nearly three lacs and eighty thousand in 5 Districts of Eastern Uttar Pradesh.

The university is located at 10 km from the historic city of Jaunpur on Jaunpur-Shahganj road which divides its 171.5 acres campus into two. Jaunpur is well connected by Train, Road and Air with the rest of the country. The infrastructure development, achievement of academic excellence, quality assurance in the higher education and socio-economic development of this highly backward & rural region of Eastern Uttar Pradesh are some of the priority areas for which the university is putting its best efforts.

Impressed with the credentials of the University, I immediately applied as it was a job in a governement University. My father who had been continuously advising me on the need of a good job as I he had to fulfil his responsibilities to see me married into a good, cultured Brahmin family of same status, was happy. He accompanied me on the day of the interview. Some fifty candidates, most of them were Ph.D. and UGC-NET, had come from long distances to appear for the interview.

When my turn came I introduced myself with all my emphasis on the need of a person who had both industry and academic experience. I felt I had satisfied the interview committee to the best of my efforts.

We returned to our village and exactly after one month the postman dispatched the letter for which my father was waiting more than me. I was selected and it was the second appointment letter of an academic assignment I had received, and that too in a government University. I got the job of lectureship on a contract basis on a salary of 8000/- a month. I was required to join before March 8, 2006.

My father was the happiest person on earth as he saw a hope for getting a high class Brahmin girl for me, which was now his primary responsibility. He again accompanied me to VBS Purvanchl University when the date of joining arrived. We stayed at the residence of one of my brother's teacher, who by then had shifted to this University as the director of the engineering college of the University. He guided both of us on the paperwork required to be submitted to the administration of the university. I started with my second academic assignment from 9th March 2006. My father advised me about the people and places in the area and left for my village – all satisfied.

Soon I got accommodation in the PG student hostel, which was primarily occupied by most of such students who were mostly interested in politics. The Head of Department was a man who had utilized all his contacts to remain in the position, but he had an academic inclination and had somehow managed to nurture a dream to grow the department.

Parmatma Mishra a fearful man who was also selected for the contract lectureship, was one whom I trusted. He was NET qualified and was enrolled for Ph.D. His biggest problem was another young and 'dynamic' entrant in the lot of contract lecturers –Digvijaya Singh. We all three were staying in the PG hostel, which was meant for students. Digvijaya Singh always barged into Parmatma's room while he would be busy talking to his would-be wife, and Parmatama would be rushing to my room to get a safe space to talk to her.

We all were happy fellows and were sure about our future and sure that like Parmatma Mishra that we would also get cultured wives. The HOD, a jack of all trades, gave me the responsibility to carry out a publication for which he allowed me to stay back till late evening. My job was to compile all the research papers which we had received from scholars in hard copy. I would read all the papers, correct them and type it them on the HOD's computer, and on Sundays I would rush to the Jaunpur town, which was 10 kms away from the university, to find a cyber café from where I could dispatch "The Nose of The News".

While on the other hand my father was busy looking out for a family where he could have tied my knot, I was enjoying the days at VBS Purvanchal University among lots of students who were keen to make an entry into the media. I was helping them out and assuring them that they all were capable individuals.

One day I received a call from my father who told me about a family who had approached him for my marriage.

In a place like eastern UP, the best way to make money is either becoming a politician or a contractor. The family who had approached my father was involved in contractorship in liaising with state government. Money was floating in that family and they were on the look out for an educated Brahmin family for their second daughter.

As in a typical higher class Brahmin family, the groom's approval matters came last while the elders of the family were to be contacted first. So, one day an arrangement was made in a lodge to see the girl to whom I was supposed to marry, after all the elders had approved the initial stages.

From my side both my elder sisters and parents, along with me, were invited while from the girl's side, the parents, her brother and his wife, and her younger sister welcomed us. The girl was educated up to my qualifications and the family, despite being contractors, was civilized.

And that is how I was engaged to a girl I hardly knew. Passing all the stages of the pre-marriage ceremony, the day came when I was supposed to be married. It was all happening within a span of one month and 18th June of 2006 was fixed for marriage.

I was the happiest person as I was getting my life-mate. Some 200 relatives from both sides participated in the marriage ceremony and in the function which lasted a day and night with the priest chanting all the hymns from the holy 'Vedas'. I was called a responsible, happily wed married man. All invitees and relatives blessed both of us for a bright future and married life.

Letters from BBC

The 2005-6 sessions at VBS Provencal had ended and gave me time to be adjusted in my new married life. But the dispatches to two media organizations and individuals including Rajdeep Sardesai and Nik Gowing had not stopped. Since it was a weekly exercise that required me to go to Faizabad city to be in a cyber café, I reduced the frequency of dispatches and tried to get feedback from the individuals who were receiving it.

The one individual who was a recipient of my dispatches was BBC news presenter and producer Lucy Hockings.

Lucy Hockings is a New Zealander who is working as a television journalist for BBC World News. She joined the network as producer in 1999, just before being promoted to senior producer in 2000, and worked on Asia Today and HARDtalk. Due to viewer complaints about her accent, she went to the Royal Academy of Drama for speech lessons. She reported on the September 11, 2001 attacks, followed by the Afghanistan and Iraq wars. In 2003, she became a presenter on BBC World (as it was then called) and covered such events as the 2004 tsunami, the death of Pope John Paul II and the 2005 London bombings. In 2006, she was made full-time presenter of The World Today. In her spare time, she is also a features reporter for BBC World News. Her previous assignments include Canada, Spain, Norway, and the Netherlands.

She currently presents the 1000UKT Newshour on BBC World News with David Eades, and bulletins at 1100UKT and 1300UKT. She can also be seen regularly standing in for Nik Gowing on weekdays to present The Hub from 1700UKT to 1900UKT broadcast every weekday on BBC World News.

I had already spoken to Nik Gowing from Thipsandara market in Bangalore. This time I was contacting Lucy Hocking. Lucy Hockings is a widely acknowledged TV presenter who appears almost daily on BBC World. The day I called BBC HQ, she was on an off day.

Now it became a routine for me to send dispatches to all the two dozen contacts every week.

And my two years effort, an unpaid 'social work' which cost me time and money both, got a reward. I received a letter from BBC HQ, which had asked me to stop mailing the BBC and to stop all communication with Lucy Hockings. The mail was more treating and less advising on the concerns I had for "The Nose of The News". I replied to them and that is how I ended my all communication and phone calls to the BBC. This was an end to "The Nose of The News", a stop to my dispatches and an end to all what I was doing in the period of joblessness which later on gave me the confidence and courage to stand tall in the market of media education. Shattered, I looked at the last communication that Tony Henningan of BBC wrote to me:

Wednesday, 27 September, 2006 2:54 PM

Tony Hennigan <tony.hennigan@bbc.co.uk> wrote:

Many thanks for your e-mail, Ratnesh and in particular might I thank you for your assurance that you will not be contacting 'BBC staff' again. I can but hope that you prove to be a man of your word and might I provide you with the assurance that you seek that I will be more than happy never to contact you ever again.

Tony Hennigan

BBC

Job hunt and Dehradun

The next session at VBS Purvanchal University had started and we were interviewed again in order to save our contractual Lecturership, but none of us was able to retain it. Parmatma Mishra shifted his base to Banaras and Digvijaya Singh filed a case on the university that a contractual lectureship which was assured for three years cannot be broken only after completion of one year. He won the case and remained in the university as contractual lecturer.

I was married by then and had an added responsibility. The reason for which I was deported from Bangalore. My father and elder brother had fulfilled their responsibility to settle me in my life. So, as a more responsible brother, he called me and my wife both to Noida. He by then had shifted to his Noida home, while he had purchased a new house in Bangalore as well.

So we boarded a train to New Delhi and landed to in the newly purchased house of my brother in Noida, in the winters of January 2007.

This time a reluctant me did not approach any individual or company in the media. The hurt before 2004, which made me leave Delhi for Bangalore, was still there. On the recommendation of my father's friend (who by now had developed a circle in Noida) I found a job as an academician in a media school of a TV Channel, which kept me engaged for the next three months.

And then I applied for a permanent lectureship with a premier institution in Dehradun, and was called for interview. This was a permanent lectureship job, with the PF getting deducted. Hurt and humiliation in Delhi made me apply for the job and in June 2007. I cleared a rather tough interview and received a four page appointment letter at my brother's residence.

This time again my father was happier than me. For the first time his son was getting a permanent job and to assure himself that I would not run away from the job, he again accompanied me to Dehradun.

The Institute of Management Studies, Dehradun was situated in the lush green area on the Dehradun–Mussoorrie road from where we could view the slope and lights of Mussoorrie. After my joining and finding a two bedroom accommodation my father had left for Noida and almost a week later my wife joined me to accompany me and to look after me. She, by then, had started understanding the problem which I had faced and I too had started listening to her. I had not been doing it so far.

We had a small department of Journalism and Mass Communication in which almost 180 students were enrolled and were taught by five faculties. All were either bachelors or newlywed or soon to be wed.

Tariq Intezar was a person who had never accepted defeat in his life. A cheerful person who had joined thein Department of Management he soon gained my confidence and became my closest friend. He had got beautiful voice and would sing 'Gazals' by putting his heart in to the song. He had finished his MBA from Aligarh Muslim University and was enrolled for a Ph.D.

Sushil Roy, a man with lots of information on current affairs, was the one who attracted my attention. He was my colleague in the Department of Journalism and Mass Communication. He had worked in media and was newlywed.

The other two people in the department were Sheel Nidhi Pandey and Vandita Tripathi. Both were the best at their area of expertise.

Dheeraj Shukla joined a couple of month later. A man who had worked in newspapers and was keenwould always to tell the stories from his family. A typically Banarsi person I often called him.

We had enough workload beyond the UGC guidelines and could would get a chance to interact with each other only in the lunch break or when college would be closed.

Traiq had been telling me stories from Aligarh and how he had a plan to go abroad after his Ph D would be over. He was one who had a very great taste about in nature and girls. He would often crack funny jokes on colleagues and even on students, but soon would become serious. Very inclined towards research activities, he presented his research paper in the conference organized by the Institute. We would, without any intention, walk towards the 'Shiv Mandir' on the upper sides of the road and would come down following the slopes on the both sides of road. Midway he would sing some Gazals or crack a joke on Dheeraj Shukla. Each evening me, Dheeraj and Tariq would go to Paltan Bazar to have 'Bun Butter' and Tariq would crack a joke on Dheeraj Shukla's addiction for 'Bun Butter'.

Soon, we discovered that we had a busy and productive life and more than this we had a workload which was going beyond our control. We had a director who was more than strict and was restless until he would not ask someone to put in his papers. Tariq would often call it 'Fall of Wicket'.

And soon the person who cracked a joke on all of us became the heart of the institute. One day when Tariq and I were having refreshments, he was called by the director. I cracked a silly joke on him when he was going to meet the director.

'Fall of All-rounder Tariq's Wicket'... I commented not knowing that it was the truth. The director had called him to put in his papers and the reason he gave was that Tariq had debarred a student who was the ward of some trustee.

Traiq was a tough man but he did not say anything, he did not counter. When he was leaving, he said to me, "Bas Itne din ki roji thi bhai" (It was a company of such few days, brother).

I was not finding Dehradun comfortable to me after Tariq had left. It appeared as if the charm, the beauty and the life had vanished from the institution.

I visited my brother in the summer of 2008 and got to know about Amity University which was expanding like a storm in the field of higher education. It had its head quarter in Noida and somehow I collected all my courage and decided to meet the Director of the communication Communication Department.

I was finding myself restless and uncomfortable in Dehradun and more over my wife was expecting. I was willing to relocate to Noida for both of our comfort. And hence, decided to go to meet to the Director of Amity School of Communication at Amity University.

Amity

Amity University, Uttar Pradesh is spread in 60 acres of land on the Yamuna Expressway, which connects Noida with Agra. It is said to be one of the finest private universities duly recognized by the state government and University Grant Commission. It now has NAAC accreditation.

Amity School of Communication is one of the premier media schools in the country which now has almost 1000 students on its roll, divided in the undergraduate, Post Graduate and Ph.D. programs.

The director of the school, a retired colonel of the Indian Army and a very disciplined man, was humble enough to give me an appointment. As the head of such a great media school he might have avoided to meeting me, but a man who knew the problems of young people gave me a chance to meet him in his office. This was a Saturday, when I went to meet him with a copy of resume. I was amazed to see a director working on Saturdays, when most of the staff and faculty were on leave. He went through my resume, asked me a couple of questions on my expertise, and instructed me to appear for a demo class.

My demo was on a Tuesday. A very optimistic me saw it as a chance to change my fate. The seven years detachment with the media hub city Delhi perhaps was gearing up to absorb me finally. I wiped off all the hurt and rejection which I had got in Delhi in 2002-2004, discussed it with my elder brother and my father, who by then had shifted his base to Noida.

On Tuesday I prepared a topic of my interest, as was suggested by the director, and went to the University. It was a working day and a dozen of faculty members were sitting to examine my expertise. I was given a half an hour time, and with all my confidence presented my lecture and answered the queries of the attendees to the best of my knowledge.

I returned to Dehradun and awaited the results. A month later I was told to face a top interview with the founder of the University, as was the culture at that time in July 2008. Initially, I was promised by the director that all would go well, and he advised me to be mentally prepared to relocate myself.

The Fonder founder of the University interacted with me in August, when he returned from a foreign trip, and finally approved my candidature to be a part of a big educational giant as a lecturer.

This was the turning point of my life, a historical moment for which I had waited for years while going through phases of disappointment and discourage. I would say the man who motivated me was the director and the person who encouraged me was my wife.

On 29th September I said fare welled to Dehradun and to IMS, and finally, along with the my father and furniture, which my father which carried my along with my luggage, I made my way to where a great and shining future was waiting for me. My wife had already come down to my brother's residence in Noida as she was in her last month of pregnancy.

The next month of joining Amity was fruitful to me as my wife delivered a healthy baby boy on October 10, 2008. The birth of Pragun, as we call him, was the happiest moment of my life and, for all of us in my family.

Amity University as expected became a turning point in my life and in my academic career. And the guiding force behind whatever I did in post the debacle days in Delhi was my mentor-like director. He brought discipline in all of us at Amity School of Communication, he brought growth and he brought happiness on each one of our faces.

Now Amity School of Communication is perhaps the largest media school in the country and has got 45 faculty members teaching almost 1000 students at the undergraduate and post-graduate level.

We work like a family and we make a team of experienced and newer group of teachers. There are some who have lots of hope, there are some who have seen the changing face of Indian media by giving their contribution to it.

Prof Kalyan Chatterjee, in whom I saw an elder brother, is an encyclopaedia of knowledge. A man with a twisting tongue, he has served both national and regional media, and came into academics just to give a change to his life and career. His political knowledge is unparalleled, his wisdom unbeaten. I continuously learn from him while arguing with him, debating with him and cracking jokes with him.

In short, Amity gave me all that I needed and gave me the courage to defeat all the failure and hurt the people and city had given me in the past. A bright day and night full of lights is ahead waiting its wings to open for me and I am ready to see the glare of success on my face.

2012 AD: End of joblessness

In the last four years of stay I developed myself from a budding media academician to one who had continuously grown. I kept doing research and presented myself twenty five times in international conferences, obtained membership of one dozen international bodies and took the responsibilities adhered to me by my University. It was a continuous learning process from colleagues, staff and family. The year 2012, which was predicted by some Mayan civilization to be the end of our world became a success for me and I attended four workshops and conferences of NASA. I was enlightened to be part of the International Space Station workshop and the Mars landing of Curiosity rover. In all of the rest of the conferences they clarified the false news of the end of the world on December 21 , 2012:

Dec 21,2012 – A Scientific Reality Check (A NASA clarification)

There apparently is a great deal of interest in celestial bodies, and their locations and trajectories at the end of the calendar year 2012. Now, I for one love a good book or movie as much as the next guy. But the stuff flying around through cyberspace, TV and the movies is not based on science. There is even a fake NASA news release out there... So here is the scientific reality on the celestial happenings in the year 2012.

Nibiru, a purported large object headed toward Earth, simply put – does not exist. There is no credible evidence – telescopic or otherwise – for this object's existence. There is also no evidence of any kind for its gravitational effects upon bodies in our solar system.

I do however like the name Nibiru. If I ever get a pet goldfish (and I just may do that sometime in early 2013), Nibiru will be at the top of my list.

The Mayan calendar does not end in December 2012. Just as the calendar you have on your kitchen wall does not cease to exist after December 31, the Mayan calendar does not cease to exist on December 21, 2012. This date is the end of the Mayan long-count period, but then – just as your calendar begins again on January 1 – another long-count period begins for the Mayan calendar.

On December 16, 1992, 8 days after its encounter with Earth, the Galileo spacecraft looked back from a distance of about 6.2 million kilometers (3.9 million miles) to capture this remarkable view of the Moon in orbit about Earth. Image credit: NASA/JPL.

There are no credible predictions for worrisome astronomical events in 2012. The activity of the sun is cyclical with a period of roughly 11 years and the time of the next solar maximum is predicted to occur about May 2013. However, the Earth routinely experiences these periods of increased solar activity – for eons – without worrisome effects. The Earth's magnetic field, which deflects charged particles from the sun, does reverse polarity on time scales of about 400,000 years but there is no evidence that a reversal, which takes thousands of years to occur, will begin in 2012. Even if this several thousand year-long magnetic field reversal were to begin, that would not affect the Earth's rotation nor would it affect the direction of the Earth's rotation axis... only Superman can do that.

The only important gravitational tugs experienced by the Earth are due to the moon and sun. There are no planetary alignments in the next few decades, Earth will not cross the galactic plane in 2012, and even if these alignments were to occur, their effects on the Earth would be negligible. Each December the Earth and Sun align with the approximate center of the Milky Way Galaxy but that is an annual event of no consequence.

The predictions of doomsday or dramatic changes on December 21, 2012 are all false. Incorrect doomsday predictions have taken place several times in each of the past several centuries. Readers should bear in mind what Carl Sagan noted several years ago; "extraordinary claims require extraordinary evidence."

For any claims of disaster or dramatic changes in 2012, the burden of proof is on the people making these claims. Where is the science? Where is the evidence? There is none, and all the passionate, persistent and profitable assertions, whether they are made in books, movies, documentaries or over the Internet, cannot change that simple fact. There is no credible evidence for any of the assertions made in support of unusual events taking place in December 2012.

Decemeber 22,2012: 07:30 AM : I woke up in my newly purchased house. My wife was sleeping alongside me, while my four year old son was in her lap. Like me everyone else woke up healthy with the new sunrays shining bright above our heads. Like me, we all were ready to welcome a new dawn, a new morning and a new hope for all of us. The world had not ended and there was a new beginning for each one of us.

I tried to believe that I had done quite enough in the last four years. The phase of failure had been wiped off. Delhi had given me a new hope, a new morning, a new day and I was ready to accept it. It was an end to my joblessness and not the end of the world.

.

Made in the USA
Middletown, DE
09 June 2021

41672440R00091